J. B. PRIESTLEY

AN INFORMAL STUDY
OF HIS WORK

J. B. PRIESTLEY

An Informal Study of his Work

BY

DAVID HUGHES

RUPERT HART-DAVIS
SOHO SQUARE LONDON
1958

Printed in Great Britain by
The Camelot Press Ltd., London and Southampton

FOR FIELDEN HUGHES

To read what one liked because one liked it, never to pretend to admire what one did not—that was his only lesson in the art of reading. To write in the fewest possible words, as clearly as possible, exactly what one meant—that was his only lesson in the art of writing. All the rest must be learnt for oneself.

Virginia Woolf, in an essay on her Father

You are likely enough, for I have seen many instances of the Sauciness of Scholars, to tell me that I am more properly employed in playing with my Kittens, than in giving myself Airs of Criticism, and censuring the Learned. But you are mistaken if you imagine I am to be intimidated by your Contempt, or silenced by your Reproofs. As I read, I have a Right to judge, and as I am injured, I have a Right to complain; and these Privileges, which I have purchased at so dear a Rate, I shall not easily be persuaded to resign.

Samuel Johnson, in a letter to The Rambler

Contents

I. Making the Introductions

I BEGIN in London: it was here, in the Charing Cross Road some years ago, that a brush with the police introduced me to the idea of one day writing a piece, perhaps even a book, about J. B. Priestley. I was standing at the shilling shelves outside a bookshop, with a copy of *Bright Day* casually in my hand and my eyes on the neat figure of a girl diminishing towards St. Martin's Lane. Someone tapped my shoulder and I swung round to find a policeman's face staring into mine. Those glances up the street, that book in my hand—a moment ago, he claimed, he had watched me slip another book into my pocket. But my pockets turned out to be empty; we gazed at each other in glassy embarrassment. However innocent I was, I felt and must have looked extremely guilty, and as the policeman grimly stifled his irritation and moved away, I continued to stand and look blankly at the opening page of *Bright Day*, the girl now forgotten as swiftly as a dream.

Then, suddenly, like nerves reawakening from the influence of drugs, one or two words on that page came alive to the eye, followed by a sentence, then a fragment of narrative. This relief, the removal of a shadow of fear represented by the law, had given the words a freshness and potency that unfolded like the coming of spring, almost as though I had been attacked by simple verbal beauty for the first time. Turning now to the third page of that book, I find: "It was full spring down there in Cornwall; and I noticed the dramatic alternations of slashing rain and sunshine, the tattered sails of cloud, the green fury of the sea, the gorse along the cliff walks and the cushions of primroses in the deep lanes; but it all seemed to be happening a long way off and to have nothing to do with me." At such words as these, the timing of moods had been perfect, I was liberated from a moment of awkward and childish fear by a handful of sentences, comforted by cushions of words. I was free to walk into the shop and buy the book, and I did so.

Coming across Priestley's books thereafter, once in Kensington, quite often in the Charing Cross Road and occasionally in those disordered bookshops that lie heaped in corners of provincial cities, I usually bought them and took them home to read. People often have absurd personal motives, far removed from critical reason in the first place, for favouring a particular author, and there is nothing wrong with that, for we make friends in the same illogical way. My introductions to Priestley were a voice heard on the wireless at the age of ten and a few words with a policeman; and on such inadequate but human foundations a long acquaintance was built. People always think a good deal about their friends, they talk, share enthusiasms and write to each other. Books, too, thrive on such intimacy, for they are changeable in the same way as people are, not fundamentally but according to mood.

A writer in whom one has found during adolescence not only something worth discovering but also the delight of discovery itself becomes, as one's life proceeds and understanding deepens, a heightened world of standards, principles and manners to which one unconsciously refers, as though he were a parent or an early environment. Sometimes the bloom of an author fades, if his values and messages prove alien to the way one has developed; his work then seems childish, merely because one has read him in childhood. It is the misfortune of a writer like Kipling, or even Kenneth Grahame, that his books become too intimately a part of growing up and are therefore almost totally renounced in maturity, except as a fond memory; and to some extent, with the generation at present in its twenties and thirties, the same thing has happened to Priestley. Most people, in their middle teens during the two decades after its publication, were launched into *The Good Companions* by parents who had bought it and kept it on their shelves, and however much they enjoyed it at the time and remember enjoying it, they still base their later estimate of Priestley, not merely on the dim recollection of a single book, but on what now seems to them the foolish uncritical admiration of a child. The case is different when, from all the possibilities jumbled together in libraries, a child selects an author for himself, sees a name he has never heard on the title-page, begins reading and is swept away. He has tripped over a secret, laid bare a new world behind the open-sesame covers of a book, and nobody else knows a thing about it: I recall a sharp disappointment when I learned on enquiry that my father had been aware of H. G. Wells's existence for years before I was born. But certainly my parents never suggested a book that I ought to read, a writer I might enjoy. I was left to find them, to pull aside curtains and feast my eyes on landscapes that had never before known human visitors.

There is no telling what hint or name or printed word will represent the beckoning finger of romance to a young mind, and I remember discovering writers quite fortuitously, because I was attracted by the colour of a binding-cloth or the rare promise of a title. Hilaire Belloc, whose name seemed to promise me somewhat outlandish pleasures, was one of the disappointments; I never really cared for his work, though I tried hard, for it was difficult to admit that my instincts were wrong, and he consequently never became a giant, looming unknowably behind his books, a legend to the fingertips. With Wells, however, I was always able to share the secret of envisaging the world in the same exclusive terms, and yet to remain quite incredulous of the existence of this wonderful figure (like Kipps, but so much wiser), who had unexpectedly tapped an answering vision in the depths of my mind. There were days when, in certain casts of light, in the atmosphere of an afternoon, I was convinced that the visible world had been, not simply observed, but actually created by Wells; his breath was in the sky. My sense of communion with him was so excited and intense that for a long time, and not at all typically, I declined to recommend his books to my friends.

I have never felt thus about Priestley, because I was first aware of him as a voice. When I first came to read a book of his, this memory of a voice persuaded me that he was a man like any other, and men are not surrounded by legends but by facts. I could not imagine Wells conducting a conversation or eating bread and butter; but Priestley, I knew, talked. Ten years old, I had been lying in the corridor of a furnished bungalow near Chichester during an air-raid when Priestley began to speak on the wireless, and I asked who it was. "J. B. Priestley," they said. "He wrote *The Good Companions*."

So it began; and it continued in the Charing Cross Road about seven years later, and it thrust itself frequently on my attention at Alton in Hampshire where we lived for some time, and it occurred to me at Oxford, and I took it with me to week-ends near Haslemere, and I brandished it at Bradford where I went to talk about it, and in London I am always finding it, just picking up a book and becoming involved for two or three hours or finding a reference and disagreeing with it: all this mirrors the slow, almost unconscious process of taking an artist into one's experience, so that he finishes by being, not a writer one has read or a painter one has looked at, but something through which one has lived, no less remarkable than a love affair. Also, in these years of developing acquaintance, one discovers the facts that have made the man as well as indulging the fancies that produce the legend. Unless they are misunderstood, which may very easily happen with a contemporary writer, both the fancies and the facts help to widen the horizons of the total experience and to deepen the comprehension of the individual books.

Here and there, from time to time, in a remark dropped casually into general conversation, by reading between the lines, by coming across passages of explicit autobiography, from books and people and newspaper articles, one discovers the facts. I found, for example, in *Who's Who* that John Boynton Priestley was born in Bradford in 1894. The son of a schoolmaster, he spent his first eighteen years in that busy black-faced city where the moors lie a few minutes walk beyond the tram-terminus. I learned that, like the young Gregory Dawson in *Bright Day*, he left school early and found

employment in a wool office, where he began to write pieces
for the local newspapers. A London editor paid him his first
guinea before he was twenty, and from that moment, although
the years of war cruelly intervened, his career was determined.
Between 1914 and 1919 Priestley served in the Duke of Welling-
ton's and Devon Regiments: five years which might in themselves have been regarded as bitter and profitless, but which
were happy of outcome in two respects. As with more than one
writer of the time, they confirmed the pre-war world as a
halcyon and deathless source of inspiration and, despite the
dangers of sentimental backward-looking and of the artificial
search for a present that could rival so apparently perfect a
past, they established for Priestley, dragged away from his
youth by war, those childlike haunts of imagination that
nourish a writer all his life. There can be little doubt that the
other outcome of those years was salutary. In 1919, on an ex-
officer's government grant, Priestley went up to Cambridge and
took a course in History and English Literature at Trinity Hall.

In 1922 the choice of a career—or at least the means of
earning a living—was still uncertain, but as might be expected
to happen with a writer hovering penniless and rather frightened on the verge of his destiny, the concrete offer of a job,
even more frightening, at once decided him. Turning down
Quiller-Couch's suggestion that he should remain at Cambridge to lecture, Priestley moved to London in 1922, "with a
young wife, no regular job and a total capital of less than fifty
pounds", and he spent the next eight years groping his way
towards the brighter lights through that slow, dusty and rather
dog-eared *demi-monde* of editorial offices and pubs round the
corner, which has swallowed up so many writers who might
have seemed at the time no less promising than Priestley. At
first he lived in Walham Green, emerging from the large-
roomed ugly flat that housed his young family into fine smoky
autumnal mornings, catching the 11 bus to Fleet Street, to
pick out a bundle of books for review or to deliver an essay; he
describes his metropolitan beginnings in an essay called
'Coming to London', recently published in a symposium of

that name. He began to be invited to parties, he worked like a
black. He wrote reviews and essays—at least one a week for
many years—and he advised a publisher, calling into the
Bodley Head every so often to flick through the manuscripts
and see which were worth taking away. He edited *The Bodley
Head Book of Verse*, and he made his discoveries. He accepted
commissions for works of criticism, adding volumes on Meredith and Peacock to Macmillan's English Men of Letters series.
He gave no sign whatever of becoming something that in
argumentative moments he has pretended to regret, a popular
best-selling novelist.

Those early years, first in Walham Green, then at Chinnor
Hill which lies between Thame and High Wycombe, and
finally back in London again in a house in Scarsdale Villas,
rise in a quick crescendo of promise to a considerable level of
achievement; they do not, however, shadow forth *The Good
Companions*. They exist as a full-scale literary career *in parvo*,
and if the eleven books by which they are represented had
been spread thoughtfully over a lifetime, I think it likely that
Priestley would have succeeded in commanding that brand of
faintly disappointed respect we reserve for authors who have
done well but little, from whom a book comes reluctantly as a
rare favour to a thirsty discriminating public. As it is, one may
say, he has written too much.

This may be said quite reasonably, for Priestley possesses
one of those infrequent minds that spring ideas from every
source, not exclusively from the inward eye. He does not, like
D. H. Lawrence for example, select plots and situations to
illustrate an intense characteristic theme; the first blood
spouts always from the objective idea, from a person or an
incident, from the immediacy of the world, and as this happens
every day to the reflective extrovert, a good number of such
ideas unfailingly take root and produce the need to write about
them. All the same, from one point of view, I doubt whether
it is true that Priestley has written too much. Unless he is
poisoned by false motives, a mature writer always strikes the
balance which his gifts and temperament qualify him for. If

for his own good he needs to stop writing for a spell, to clear the air or prepare for the breaking of new ground, then he will always do so involuntarily—and probably much to his annoyance. Priestley is an impulsive unpremeditative author, in the power of his zestful talents. He has ever been subject to the periodic monsoon of ideas, conceptions and inspirations, and his land has been irrigated to deal with it. Not unnaturally, the more he writes the more an author lays himself open to books that are below his highest level, and thus, in some years, the crop may be said to have failed. Failures are remembered for the distasteful and unworthy reason that successes cannot be forgotten.

I was recently told that *The Good Companions* was born one morning in the offices of the *London Mercury* when Sir John Squire, who had a sound editorial instinct for tapping sources in an author of which the latter himself was unaware, turned to Priestley and ordered him to begin on the following morning a long picaresque novel. Whether this tale is true hardly matters, though it is more pleasant to contemplate a writer stumbling on a gold-mine rather than, as people often assume, deliberately setting out to capture fame and fortune. But however true in spirit, it is certainly untrue in fact, for early in 1927, more than a year before he wrote the opening sentences of the novel, Priestley told his agent that he had a sort of humorous-romantic epic in mind. Even so, it is unlikely that Priestley knew what he was doing when he started work on *The Good Companions*, for acceptance has at last been found for the (to writers) irritating truth that public taste cannot be conscientiously tracked and netted: it is the butterfly that always flutters out of reach. Writers are rarely conscious of the implications, on any level from the public attitude to the deepest meaning, of a piece of writing on which they are currently engaged. Somerset Maugham expresses the view, in *The Summing-Up*, that writers do not have to be particularly intelligent to produce fine work—perhaps even work which, if it came from the pen of another, they would not fully understand—and although Priestley relies unusually much on the

fluency and drive of his intelligence in shaping his artistic
purposes, his intelligence is certainly not of the kind that
soberly plans a neat future. Maugham himself has calculated
the direction of his career and the appeal of his work with a
much sharper degree of shrewdness than Priestley could ever
summon, with his almost boyish enthusiasm for the idea of the
moment.

In a summary of a man's career as brief and introductory as
these first paragraphs, it is somewhat difficult to avoid all
mention of trends and turning-points; to me this form of
generality is exciting, but it cuts no critical ice. I will therefore
simply record that in 1928, when he moved house from Church
Hanborough in Oxfordshire to Well Walk in Hampstead,
Priestley fled from his quiet bookish study of literary essays and
short highly-charged novels of atmosphere, into the open
world of more vigorous polemic and big lively novels of character and adventure. And soon after that, in 1932 when his study
was Coleridge's bed-sitting room in a house in Highgate
Village, he provided another excuse for indicating a turning-
point by writing *Dangerous Corner* and beginning to give his
serious (and for long stretches undivided) attention to the
drama. Today Priestley regards himself as primarily a
dramatist.

In 1933 Priestley acquired Billingham Manor in the Isle of
Wight and he built a study on the roof which, like the bridge
of a ship, commanded a view of half the island; and at the same
time as he was succumbing to the temptations of the growing
world of films, writing stories for Michael Balcon at Gaumont-
British and for Gracie Fields, he was also busy with plays. The
thirties were devoted chiefly to the drama, and the plays in
which he is often startlingly seen at his best belong to that
uneasy period before the second war. We, the generation that
has grown up since that war, find it hard to acknowledge the
Priestley handed down to us in the murmur of gossip paragraphs and, more negatively still, in the dictates of current
fashion, as a writer addicted to experiment and responsible for
innovation. Once again, it seems, the extreme success of one

book brands him, with an injustice equal to that success, as a
solid traditionalist who made an attempt, in currying public
favour, to drag our bright progressive literature back into the
mists where the jolly spirits of Fielding, Smollett and Dickens
eternally dance. It is none the less a fact that Priestley's work,
especially in the theatre, is experimental in the way ambitious
content is adapted to the harsh demands of form; only a master
of stagecraft and an original approach could have constructed
such firm and disciplined plays out of the riotous material that
went to the making of *I Have Been Here Before* and *Music at
Night*. In his prose, too, the thirties produced a minor but most
successful experiment in autobiography. *Midnight on the Desert*
and its successor, *Rain Upon Godshill*, are regarded by some
people as his most natural, ranging and satisfying books. A
third volume had been planned and part-written when the war
intervened.

The books Priestley wrote during the war sprang intimately
from the occasion and are steeped in the electric, challenging
and oddly beautiful atmosphere of that time, particularly of
the first tense summer of war when his *Postscripts* were broadcast. Therefore, like much occasional work, they can be valued
only by reference to history, not in this case to the facts of
history but to a remembered atmosphere. A novel like *Blackout
in Gretley*, with its almost archaic title, exudes a kind of period
flavour which must condition its impact on readers coming to
it for the first time today; it is tense and curiously unreal like a
melodrama of the eighteen-seventies, yet in a way its deep
immersion in the bleak weather of wartime circumstances
improves it. It offered the relief of escapism and not, like most
of Priestley's work, a view of reality: a view which, though it
may often seem superficially cheery, plumpened by the yeast of
an irrepressible personality, is actually touched with gloom,
with that same sort of exuberant pessimism that frequently
makes the mood and attitude of poets difficult to determine. At
the same time, despite this view, it would be wrong to fall a
prey to the facile temptation of taking Priestley as a prophet
of gloom. He should not perhaps be regarded as a prophet at

B

all, however fond he is of strong statement and prognosis. The right of a man of letters to preach has never been denied, provided he is liberal in sugaring the pill, and I do think it true that Priestley's opinions are sometimes too powerfully felt to make the necessary sugar seem more to him than a decadent luxury.

After the war, partly for political reasons perhaps, that slight edge of misinterpretation, that slackening of the true critical focus, has crept into the fashionable, though probably not the public, estimate of Priestley. In 1949, when already for some years he had been dividing his time between chambers in Albany and his house in the Isle of Wight, he wrote *Delight*, one of his most disarming and thoroughly likeable books of essays. Prefacing the book with what he calls "The Grumbler's Apology", Priestley takes some trouble to explain the popular view of him as a man on whom the burden of life is almost too heavy for hope or patience. Yet that view persists. In 1951 he published his last enormous novel (the fifth), *Festival at Farbridge*, and although one may doubt whether it is among his most notable books, its author did not deserve the reputation of a jovial, back-slapping and quite unrealistic fellow that has since been established by critical suggestion in the popular mind. The fact that these two views of Priestley clash so violently should be sufficient to expose them as superficial. They cannot both be true; and yet they are—though not exclusively, not entirely. The truth is that they have a bearing on the truth, and that there is a good deal more. In the course of these pages—though I wish it could be done by an instantaneous flash of persuasion—we will find out what more exists.

Priestley is in his early sixties, and I am moving towards thirty. Most of my reading has been done in London, for I have lived there, with periods away, since I was sixteen; it cannot have been long after we moved from the country that I was almost arrested in the Charing Cross Road. The facts about Priestley—date of birth, lists of books, hobbies, addresses and chairmanships—are to be found in skeleton by opening a copy of *Who's Who* in any library, and the books catalogued there can usually be borrowed. For two summers now I have managed a good deal of reading during week-ends at a small pub which lies off the main road between Midhurst and Haslemere in Sussex; one always has two or three books in one's zip-bag, even if the week-end is hot and we play cricket in the pine-woods. I read extensively at Oxford too, neglecting the syllabus with deliberate folly; I recall Priestley being interviewed for the *Isis*, lying heavily on his bed in the Mitre and talking about the play he had just written with Jacquetta Hawkes, *Dragon's Mouth*. Nowadays I go in the summer to Chideock, which is in Dorset, where the hills lie close to Hardy; last time the land was drugged with heat and only honeysuckle flavoured the air, and I remember sending down a parcel of Priestley's books so large that the Post Office was longing to refuse it.

I make no apology for offering these facts, for I believe it is important to recollect how and where and why one read certain books and was moved by various experiences. Remembering a book and judging it is like returning to a haunt of the mind, a place where something happened, a corner of thought and feeling which now belongs to the past; and these parts of the mind which hold books safe long after they have been read contain also a memory of the deckchair in the sun, the afternoon when you telephoned the office and pretended to be ill, the night when you were too queasy with love to sleep, and rushed into a book like a drunkard. Time and place: they alter the look of a book and make judgment uncertain.

But now I am in London. A basement room in Porchester Terrace is fitted out as a study, which the sun visits slantingly for only an hour every evening; even so, I find I can both write and read in it. But I do too little of both. I thought the other day how actively Priestley lived, sometimes according to belief, often at the behest of caprice. That is perhaps, though, too light a word to convey the mood in which he will decide to undertake a particular piece of work, but earlier I implied the rather planless course of his literary production which induces him to accept—not "what the public wants", in Arnold

Bennett's dangerous phrase—but whatever fresh adventure in writing crops up in his creative intelligence. His work can be divided, not too untidily, into the inspirations that drifted his way inevitably but without warning (the right idea magically hitting the right moment), the books which his social conscience or his sense of artistic responsibility have dictated (books battered out for an occasion which vary in merit), and the notions, as opposed to ideas, which diverted him in their sudden advent but never really got under way. An instinctive, fluent and energetic writer like Priestley never examines, with the care to which Flaubert subjected his ideas, the creative diseases which develop from a casual germ almost more quickly than his mind can control them. This is not to say that he does not work out in detail his plots and stories; it is merely to suggest that Priestley is capable of letting an idea slip past him which is not quite true to the particular nature of his gifts, which he has chosen for some specious reason (in *Three Men in New Suits* this reason is political), or from which he has already squeezed every ounce of juice in a previous book.

Compton Mackenzie has written more than one book a year for the whole of his life: these statistics include the cradle. Although Priestley cannot rival this massive performance— the first war made him a late starter—his books stand impressively in front of me along this desk, most of them bound in navy-blue and lettered in gold. I suppose that if they were piled on top of each other, they would reached a man's height, a miniature toppling pagoda of books, based on the thick solid foundations of *Angel Pavement* and *The Good Companions* and rising to gay trifles like *Talking* and *Brief Diversions* at the top. Priestley's work would fill a trunk, form a parcel that the Post Office would most certainly refuse, pleasantly furnish a chilly guest-room. Ships' libraries, Aldous Huxley says somewhere, are bought by weight; the weight of Priestley would satisfy a purser that he had done well by his ship. One of the difficulties in assessing Priestley's general worth as a writer is that he has made contributions to literature at so many levels, from the plain thriller to the philosophical enquiry into the nature of time, that one will discover a book or two of his with equal probability accompanying Proust and William Nicholson in a Wiltshire drawing-room as among the tattered paper-backs of a ship's library. There cannot be many places where one would find his complete works assembled together. Even in his own house they are not. They are, however, thanks to a too zealous policeman, here in Porchester Terrace, and I hope in these pages.

II. A Personal Writer

FOR more than twenty years Priestley has lived on the Isle of Wight, and the first of his openly personal books, *English Journey*, was written just when he was on the point of moving to the island for the first time, in 1933. This rough-edged diamond of land, a jewel set in a sea that only occasionally seems silver, was regarded by the Victorians as a sort of home-spun Capri, a resort where the airs were smilingly healthy; and the strip of sea which defended the island against the vulgar invasions of the mainland must have given it a faintly foreign, even exotic flavour in the eyes of those who, like Tennyson and the Queen, prosperously retreated to its expansive manors. Even today the journey is awkward—at least to the west of the island where the beaches are empty and the downs less interrupted by the respectable box-like architecture that littered Hampshire at the turn of the century with houses for retired policemen. Nowadays a sprinkle of watering-places conta-minates the eastern coastline with pin-tables, ugly boarding-houses and picnic-refuse fluttering in the sand. These, no less than Southsea or Hayling, are the suburbs of Portsmouth, and the popular weight falls on the eastern side.

But as one moves west, past the landslide at Blackgang on the southern tip and along the military road that was built to deal with Napoleon, the country deepens and the distances become remote, the downs swell tranquilly away from the cliffs, and the upland pasturage gives way here and there to forests of pine or a bright acreage of gorse and heather. None of the many subtly differing types of country in the island lasts for long, and before one has realised what a deep whisper of silence the sea-winds must bring to these hills, one has moved

22

past them into Freshwater and the brick villas staring self-righteously out to sea. Seven miles from Yarmouth and three from Freshwater stands Brook Hill, a house where the routine of living proceeds as quietly and comfortably as a sheep, although, seen from a distance, it wears the somewhat vulpine clothing of a fortress. One can often detect in J. B. Priestley, who occupies that house, a tendency to regard himself as the sheep who is forced by the condition of society or the state of the world to appear in the wolf's clothing of anger and invective, and even apart from that he has much in common with the solid commanding house where he lives.

Priestley is a public figure, as Wells and Chesterton were, as Dickens was; he is a public figure who has tried to establish himself by honest means in an age increasingly dominated by the public personality put over in brief neonlit glimpses and the exaggerated shouts of modern publicity methods. Because these methods are unfavourable to serious men, most writers have slipped out of the public scene and try to do their work quietly back-stage. Graham Greene is a figure one rarely sees or hears tell of, as he travels more or less incognito about the world, never staying for long in one place; Joyce Cary shyly inhabited a house in North Oxford; not long ago H. E. Bates somewhat shamefacedly admitted that he preferred to be left alone with a gramophone in a comfortable room. Our best writers are drawn with reluctance and infrequency into public affairs; they so seldom sit on committees or make pronouncements on matters that do not directly concern them that newspaper controversies sometimes try to arouse them to a deeper sense of engagement in the perilous circumstances of our time. But they are not in retreat, these writers. Their silence is a token of their concern, a proof that they have found the freedom to observe and comment in their own way.

Priestley, however, is a writer nourished in an earlier tradition in which a man of letters increased his dignity and value to the community by being also a man of affairs; he is and always has been involved in the current scene. When he grapples with a political issue it is not a case of poking his nose into other people's business, although it can be interpreted as such, but rather the result of a not unreasonable belief that a writer, articulate and detached, can see that issue in an individual and also possibly a useful and clarifying way. This is not interference: the writer's place is in society, and he is by vocation a servant. The fact that he is self-appointed and working alone may be expected to touch off a certain resentment in a democratic community when what he says is wayward or unpopular. "I try to examine the world", Priestley writes in *Thoughts in the Wilderness*, "from the standpoint of a man, more fortunate than many others, who can afford to tell an unpleasant truth or two, not having a boss to please, a job to lose. This is one advantage of being a writer: you can venture, though not of course without risk, to blurt out the truth now and again."

These risks cannot be helped. But if we give an author credit in his fiction for an observant eye, a gift for recognising the bones of a situation behind its swollen and distorted flesh, and powers of deduction about the irregular and unpredictable pattern of human life, then we should extend that credit to his public utterance on political or social matters. Almost anyone will find a number of his views unacceptable and too frequently expressed, but they represent a cautiously developed system of thought about this life which owes its value to the fact that he does not require that extreme detachment cherished by many of his contemporaries.

THAT RICH INVOLUNTARY MEMORY

Apart from the early essays Priestley has written five personal books. *English Journey* was an attempt to discover how the economic crisis of the thirties had affected this country, and it was written in the most relaxed and carelessly unconscious style that Priestley had yet discovered. Of all his books this is the closest he approaches to journalism, and it is possible to argue that because he was concentrating with fierce attention on the outward scene and trying to convey that scene truthfully and not merely record his own reactions to it, he was therefore indirectly revealing more of himself than in the more explicitly personal volumes that followed. For a scene is always tilted significantly by a writer's imagination, however urgent his quest for the clean unimagined truth, and when he believes in the dispassion of his eye, he is performing the act of integration between his subject-matter and himself without thinking about it. But if his intent is avowedly personal, he is not only apt to dramatise himself, casting a disproportionate figure in the mould of his prose, but is also liable to be blind to some of the simplest facts that occur to other people about him or to invent and develop traits of literary character which do not actually exist at all. A writer need never feel guilty about promoting such apparent deception. A literary personality is justified in being built up as inventively as a work of fiction since the author's purpose is almost invariably similar in each case, to convey the attitudes and opinions natural to his vision through the medium of a narrative. He can therefore take any steps within the bounds of consistency to ensure that the expression of his mind is given the most dramatic chance to reach the surface, even to the extent of pointing his own temperament to emphasise his beliefs. In this respect Priestley's two most dramatic books were the two volumes of autobiography published in the years before the war: *Midnight on the Desert* in 1937 and *Rain Upon Godshill* two years later.

These books are both constructed on the same blueprint, and in laying out his plan Priestley was concerned, as always, to give himself as much scope as possible without letting the form burst open at the seams. His intention was to create an opportunity to range as discursively as he felt inclined over the whole of his experience without being committed to the rather limiting disciplines of a chronological pattern. He had no wish to tell the story of his life; events never interest him so much as experience, and experience is valuable for what it spontaneously suggests to his mind. He was also aware that the most disarming way of asserting one's personality agreeably in what might be thought an impossibly egocentric book was to make a projection of oneself, not to write as though one were inextricably involved with the past but almost to make it appear that one was describing in affectionate but not uncritical terms the mind and spirit of another person. Priestley achieves this end by establishing two quite separate but none the less integrated personæ, two Priestleys existing at different times and set in two different actions.

In *Midnight on the Desert* the first present-tense Priestley is sitting in his Highgate study on a dark wet Monday morning, writing the very words that we are reading and acting as controller and judge of the other Priestley who, some months before, had spent a night brooding, smoking and sorting papers in a small wooden shack on the Arizona desert. What he thought, dreamed, decided that night, the incidents he recalled, the grievances and frustrations he aired, the moments that enchanted him or left him in despair, all these are the story of the book, puffing out of the narrative as lazily as spirals of tobacco smoke. They curl into the air and seem to disappear but leave the room filled with an unmistakeable personal atmosphere. But all the time the Priestley sitting in Highgate is busy filtering the images and thoughts, putting them into order and finding a perspective for them by the very act of memory, so that the personality of the writer may be said to exist, at any one moment, at three different times: in the act of experiencing, then in the process of recalling that experience on the reflective bright-starred night in Arizona, and finally as he puts the recollecting pen to paper in the gloom of his study in London.

Roughly the same plan guides *Rain Upon Godshill*. Here Priestley is describing the events that occurred after he returned from that winter in Arizona, and with the klaxon of approaching war in his ears, he spends a day drifting vaguely along the tide of his thoughts (when he ought to be working) in the study high on the roof of his first house in the Isle of Wight, Billingham Manor. The five big windows which commanded such a sweeping view across the island over green downs and woodland dripping with rain form the coign of vantage from which

Priestley can make his broad surveys of the ideas that have bothered him, the events that crowded his time and the political or social tangles that he seeks an opportunity to discuss. We are made to feel that this is an informal chat in which, pacing that study and lighting our own pipes, we are expected to disagree sharply and find a point of view for ourselves.

Every writer would ideally like to sell his opinions in bulk to an avid set of disciples, people who go through the world like dancing images of himself to cast their influential shadows on the turn of events and the climate of thought. But no writer expects it, and sometimes even the most patient of them (and Priestley does not fall into that class) lose heart and temper at the spectacle of so many wasted words that leave the world unmoved and unchanged. What writers do have a right to expect, however, is that their words should be the thin end of the wedge, prising open a gap in shut minds and setting to work the wheels within. Priestley, by using every device of verbal mischief-making consistent with a sound argument, almost dares you to disagree with him, and the wide margins provided by these volumes tempt the scribbling of angry notes.

So Priestley at last has begun to talk. He had started by hiding his face behind the wax artificial hand of the early essays, peeping out now and again but finding that the sound of his own voice made him somewhat self-conscious. He had then for a number of years concealed himself quite successfully behind the close-packed narratives of the novels, allowing one or two attitudes to creep between the characters and make themselves public but never pushing the spectacle of life wholly aside to give himself greater freedom to talk about it. Then the plays began to appear, and at first he kept firmly in the gloom at the back of the dress-circle where no one should see him, while the characters on the stage were permitted to convey a few discreet whispers of the man who had created them. *English Journey* in 1934 loosened his tongue, but indirectly it was *The Good Companions* that dragged him out of the private corners and small back rooms where writers distractedly wait until the cry goes up for them. For now Fleet Street set about him, and it was assumed that because he had written a novel which everyone liked his words on any topic under the sun were worth several shillings apiece.

Readers, whose idle curiosity about the habits and views of authors they favour would be better replaced by a genuine concern to honour them like statesmen, always feel cosier when they are on terms of sufficient acquaintance with a public figure to recognise him in the street and run home breathlessly with the news. To the English there is something faintly scandalous about fame, and even if it makes a man more legendary, every new statement or appearance in public knocks one more nail into the coffin of his respectability. We are a childlike people in the sense that we never quite trust anyone who is not precisely like us, and we take pleasure in believing ill of the mighty because it is something of a relief. A writer who expects notice to be taken of a forceful article he has contributed to the popular press would be better occupied in confining his work to the intelligent weeklies; the English may believe everything they read in the newspapers, but they do not trust it. Friends are won and people influenced only when they are told what they already know to be true.

Priestley has perhaps suffered less from this complacency than others (they sniggered at Shaw's pronouncements because he ate vegetables and lived too long, and Wells was always a mischievous scaremonger too clever by half), for Priestley himself gives the comfortable impression of complacency. Here was a man, solidly built, hailing from the tough reliable north, liking nothing more than a quiet pipe by the fire, who would never cut a dash for its own sake or eccentrically pull the public's leg. It was felt at first that if you managed to rouse this paternal good-natured figure from his armchair doze he would say something that the family might find safely amusing. Although at the time his audience ranged through every class of society and all levels of intelligence, very few people regarded him as an intellectual whose inquisitive eye, planted on the scene around him, never rested for a moment. By sometimes oversimplifying an issue to make its outlines clear to a wide audience, Priestley kept active the development of his public identity as a plain man with a few homely words to say, and that made him invaluable during the war when people were prepared to take comfort from anyone who could find words for their anxiety. The less happy result of this, however, was that after the best-selling novels nobody quite knew where to find him.

In a back street of Bristol they read *The Good Companions* and the *Daily Express*: what could they be expected to make of the experimental time plays? A doctor in a Hamsphire village read *Angel Pavement* and the *New Statesman*: did Priestley really write *Let the People Sing* and those superficial snatches of comment on anything from divorce to the international situation that one saw in the popular dailies? A dilettante in Kensington read the early criticism and the *Criterion*: had Priestley not (quite plainly) gone to pieces in playing the somewhat pretentious game of writing down to the masses and keeping the middle class people contented? For none of these people—or at least for the classes they represent—could Priestley ever again hit the nail squarely on the head; he was always changing course, zigzagging between them as if determined to throw them off balance. Ever since the middle of the thirties, it has (not unreasonably) become the habit to approach a new work by Priestley in a watchful and suspicious frame of mind, so that when he is praised the approval is even more valuable than it seems and when he is blamed the criticism was waiting there to spring out all the time. The fact is that his true personality, as an artist, as a thinker and as a man, has never been established as a whole, and it is therefore customary either to reject his attitudes at a glance or to misinterpret them according to a preconceived and probably false image of Priestley. Nobody is to blame for this, but writers are always worth following even when they lead us a dance (probably more so than if they merely take a measured predictable walk with us), and it is easier to do this when we are sure of the character and temperament behind the work. Only then may one be excused for

committing the discourtesy of rejection or the error of misinterpretation.

A BOLD FRONT TO THE WORLD

A journey through England, a constant dalliance for several
busy years with the newspaper world, frequent appearances
on public platforms: in the early thirties all these brought
Priestley closer to the people for whom he wrote as well as to
the kind of approach and style in his writing that would
perform the same office, without recourse to conscious art, without being untrue to himself. The manner of his early writing
shows a buoyant devotion to the humours of words, a delight
in language for its own sake that ran contrary to his by no
means poetic instinct for words, but as time went on he began
to use words more as a means of supporting unobtrusively the
sense they contained, than as a power working in its own right
to decorate and enrich the meaning. Every sentence could
contain a touch of drama in the way it was constructed to add
spice to the sense, but it must not look proud of its literary up-
bringing. The basic mood of self-revelation must be relaxed,
scrupulously honest and as natural and unlicensed as the flow of
private thought. The purpose of thinking is to discover the
truth by taking our experience to pieces and reassembling it in
a more logical design, and of all human activities it is the one
that requires the most humble approach. Autobiography may
sometimes seem a particularly egocentric way of appearing in
print, but in fact the best autobiographical writing is entirely
modest; the writer is concerned to make explorations through
the self rather than of it.

That is why thought instead of incident occupies pride of
place in *Midnight on the Desert* and its successor. With observations on the passing scene and events in his private life, Priestley
encloses his more static discussions within the frame of a
narrative; in the same way the act of thinking in an express
train speeds the processes of the mind and colours them with
impressions of a fleeting landscape. At the same time, to give

his reflections root and a proper relation to the personal characteristics that govern them, he refers the reader constantly back
to himself, his habits of mind, standards long held and the shape
his life has taken. Thought never exists in a void but is stimulated by the mood of a mind at a particular moment when
certain things are happening; there are very few matters, if we
live progressively, about which nothing could persuade us to
change our minds. When there are many it means that we have
ceased to ask questions.

An aggressive manner that seems to brook no contradiction
hardly suggests that Priestley's mind is free to chop and change,
to rove in pursuit of new answers to all the old questions. In
the tradition of brusque northcountrymen who seem to know
their own minds, he is impatient of doubt and uses strong speech
to persuade his hearers that, however much they waver in their
opinions, he is as firm as a rock—while above the unquestion-
ing voice are the shrewd and sensitive eyes of a man who knows
that nothing remains unaltered for long. Besides, people always
listen to other people's certainties because they are so anxious
to find some of their own. "I have the kind of temperament
that tends to go against the company it is keeping", he says in
Midnight on the Desert. "It is as if my instinct is always towards
restoring some lost balance. Actually I have few definite beliefs
of my own, and not even the ghost of a systematic philosophy
of life." This is not to say that we should take his pronouncements warily, but just to emphasise that he is engaged in
exploration and not discovery, and that if we agree with his
findings we do so at our own risk. He says, in speaking of the
state of the world, that there are two ways of dealing with such
subjects, either to keep yourself out of all the doubts and difficulties you report in the artful and impressive manner that
H. G. Wells achieved, or "not to pretend any detachment and
superiority, to be frankly in the muddle yourself, and to be
easy and personal. This suits my temperament which has
nothing of the grand and prophetic about it."

Through both these books we learn a good deal about
Priestley's temperament; he realises that the effect of what he

has to say depends upon our understanding of it, and of course it is always comforting to write about oneself after barking one's shins for so long on the sharp edges of imaginary characters. And what do we learn? He is neither very astute nor very observant, he is inclined to be timid, irresolute, melancholy; he is easily influenced and frequently humbugged; he has neither the enterprise nor the determination to be a hard careerist. Again, he takes no thought whatever about a career, makes no plans far ahead, but does whatever he wants to do with no reference to its possible dignity or lack of it. He has a restless nature, easily bored, and so flits from one kind of work to another (for he has always wanted vaguely to be an all-round man of letters on the eighteenth-century plan). He has his hobby like another, and it happens to be the search for wisdom. He came out of the war determined to over-act, if anything, the part of the comfortable bourgeois in slippers. He is more intuitive than shrewd (the adjective frequently applied to him by reviewers), and his method is to observe closely and sharply and then guess, rather than to tabulate and reason. He has always held that in all good literature there is a certain satisfying balance of sharp criticism of our common life and an escape from it.

His appearance, he says, resembles that of a gigantic and apoplectic frog talking with a broad Yorkshire accent. As a novelist, working in a medium that has no special attraction for him, he has often been guilty of writing *down*, of an easy negligence, but in the drama, the form of writing he most enjoys, he is at once boldly experimental and extremely conscientious. His habitual mood when alone is rather sombre and brooding, which does not mean that he fakes his writing when it takes on a hearty, bustling, zestful manner. There is about him a certain charming or, if you are feeling like that, irritating naïveté, and he really dislikes being on show although he is one of those persons who are stimulated rather than frightened and frozen by an audience, despite a nervousness at the thought of appearing in public. It is one of his virtues as a listener that he enjoys a massive and probably monstrous generalisation for its own sake, and he has always had a greedy, sensual, gorging habit with beautiful sound so that he has spent whole days in the recurring rhythm of one little tune. He is always alternately being a fine fellow, armoured in self-esteem, and a second jeering self that disarms and then kicks out the fine fellow. He is not a man of destiny; he follows no star; no angelic voices guide him; he lives, like the majority, in an earthly muddle.

Out of such words as these the man begins to take shape, and in the way his mind moves by easy association from one topic to another he reveals still more of the temperament that governs the thought. No ideas are yoked by violence together; the changes of mood, tempo and subject are always casually made at precisely the right moment because Priestley is apt to grow bored a fraction before the reader will. The intellectual range is surprising, and ideas are cultivated sensibly so that, if their abstract subtleties are never picked out and labelled but only indicated in a vague untechnical way, neither are such ideas ever withdrawn from the immediate application to life which is Priestley's sole concern with them. He enters politics with the grim humour of a man who realises that he will be told that he is treading on specialist ground and has no idea what he is talking about; but there he is, suddenly, strolling round the perimeter of the arena like a banderillero and keeping his eye resolutely fixed on the unpredictable antics of the bull.

A belief in some form of socialism, he says, is not an act of rebellion with him but almost something that belongs to tradition and filial piety, and probably for that reason he has always shown an intense unwillingness to join forces whole-heartedly with any political party. He admits that one can be too easy and cheerfully cocksure in advocating reforms, redefinitions and revisions of attitude when the high stakes one is playing for are not those of the political scene where the rolling of logs and racing of rats are the tricks that win the game. But his stakes are in a way higher and he is playing no less responsibly, for he is discovering through the thickets of political theory the conditions of living in a modern state which best suit the English temperament, and he looks continually for the

c

speediest, if not the most likely, way of getting there. His arguments are always neat, persuasive and very strongly felt. If one distrusts the Liberal Socialism—one of the most indefinite terms in politics—which keeps a man out in the no-man's-land snarling at the parties and exhorting the people to use their minds creatively, there are passages in these books which absolutely vindicate the kind of original independent thinking which makes any system of government almost impossible to run but at the same time keeps it alive, progressive and close to the people. These two books were in line with the conditions of the time; they also went beyond those conditions. Times have changed since then, and Priestley's modification of his political views (though the basic principles remain unchanged) is to be found in *Thoughts in the Wilderness*.

Priestley has the type of obstinate mind which refuses to accept what appears established until he has proved to his own satisfaction that there is still a good deal of life in it. For example, "our commonest error of speech is our description of this country as a democracy; we are not a democracy, but a plutocracy roughly disguised as an aristocracy". Parliament is examined, the skeleton of the social structure revealed (and shown to be in the cupboard); he moves intelligently through economics, ideologies, ways of life; he gives birth, with the utmost caution but with a warmth of enthusiasm as well, to the bright Utopia his thoughts have trifled with at odd idealistic moments. But "the typical English mind mistrusts clearcut formulas, a logical pattern, severely rational boundaries, and likes to move delicately in a slight haze", and fortunately for their humanity and wisdom, their sense of a person still amazed and at large in the mystery of the world, the haze never quite clears from *Midnight on the Desert* and *Rain Upon Godshill*. Dogmatic and insufferable as they often appear in their forthright denunciations and almost insolent buttonholing of the reader who has done Priestley no harm, they are basically shy and irresolute books that merely try very hard to be honest, stimulating and useful. Over *Midnight on the Desert* hangs a haze of sweet American tobacco smoke, and the hazy mists of a moist English spring in the Isle of Wight drift across every page of *Rain Upon Godshill*. They are books as conscious that life remains always a secret, books as firmly set in society as any of Priestley's creative work, and they are equally close to the questing astonished imagination, a child's mind wondering at the world, which redeems even his least satisfactory work from total failure.

For they travel far, these volumes, away from ideas and in search of adventure. They cross the American continent in trains, pause hectically in New York, drive down the long boulevards of the western seaboard and come up for long periods into the rare beautiful landscapes of desert, canyon and prairie. They wander down the heat of the Nile in boats and drift back in time to stare open-mouthed at the ancient worlds. They are busy in London, moving among people and public events, turning their back for a moment on streets, theatres, telephones and occupying a sudden silence of private thought. They hover over the exquisite, blossom-filled landscapes of southern England where the island sparkles of spring days. In the turn of every tide a flotsam of magic is washed up on the shore, a few discoveries that leave one speechless, an adventure that no one could have predicted. As Priestley says of something else, "this is not a plain realism, but a realism merging into the magical". Behind the clear objective observations and the people and countrysides jumbled into racy pictures like a movie, behind the descriptions are the eyes that have been brightened by them. Priestley enjoys that kind of perception of life which always remains incredulous of what it sees, and knows that the mystery, whatever manifestations erupt from it across the surface of the earth, lies beyond all understanding. Yet still he must try to understand it, and every corner turned in the search for knowledge finds the mouth dropping still wider open in awe. Nothing can be taken for granted, and even if the mind can grapple tolerably well with the oddities of the world that the eyes observe, the spirit is often made so drunk by romance, the "call to the essential nature, the innermost self", that the only answer is silence.

THESE SMALL AMENDS

But it is between the covers of *Delight,* published in 1949, that Priestley really gives in to this intoxication, this reeling of the spirit which the wonders of the world have caused in him. This book is a collection of one hundred and thirteen brief essays, moments of experience captured on the wing, as ethereal as bluebirds but as common as rooks, memories and impressions of delight. Priestley has always been a grumbler and in his preface he puts forward the reasons for it: in the West Riding "all local customs and prejudices favour the grumbler"; he has always held that a fine grumble makes things better rather than worse; a writer should always come out critically and tell the truth, and he has grumbled in print more on other people's behalf than on his own; a fortunate man in many respects, some of his fault-finding has been a determined avoidance of *hubris.* Therefore, to make direct amends to the family who had for so long suffered from "the old glum look and the thrust-out lower lip", he captured and recorded these moments when the dark veil of this awkward, gloomy and disturbing life lifted for a second and briefly showed the more beautiful face beneath.

Fountains. That is the first sentence of the book. Then there are reading detective stories in bed, the sense of release from prison when a long difficult piece of work has been accomplished, entering a cinema one drenched afternoon in Golders Green to discover the Marx Brothers, scenting land on the air after the long vague dream of an ocean voyage, listening to chamber music at home, rummaging through other people's books and music in furnished houses, the moment when the house lights fade or the orchestra tunes up, blossom and bass voices, making stew and frying potatoes in the open air, tasting certain kinds of morning and indulging certain shameful attitudes. If life is composed of moments, most of which slip past us almost unnoticed because we are trivially busy or blindly anxious, then these are the times when we pause and are suddenly aware of this rich deep world we have inherited. We are so thankful for the reminder because we might so easily have forgotten; we do not know whether to laugh or cry.

These pieces represent the perfection to which all Priestley's early acquaintance with the essay has brought him; he has reached the easiest intimacy with the form and for that reason passes from the first word into a most disarming intimacy with the reader, striking the note of fellow-feeling without affectation or the false camaraderie that can so readily get hold of an essay and make it squirm. Each piece runs to the length it requires, some less than a page, others developing from point to point in a crescendo that leads to a climax of delight at the end. His work, he says, has always aimed at a certain eagerness and sweep and though these qualities have sometimes led him into hasty and careless writing when his style was not sufficiently stimulated by the content, they carry his somewhat workaday prose far off the ground when his heart is in the matter. The effects in *Delight* are always beautifully and naturally timed to bring the reader to the same moving unexpected twist of happiness that Priestley once felt in secret and is now concerned to share. We hack our way through the tangled undergrowth of problems and irritations, sweating and whining with the bother of life, until suddenly there we are, in the open air, with a scene of unparalleled charm and wonder before us. A moment of exquisite order follows hours of chaos; after battling long against wind and weather we achieve a moment of calm. Priestley's natural instinct is to provide the balance, to throw in his weight on the unpopular side, to even things out a little. It is why he has always been in opposition: no bandwagons for Priestley. And now, perhaps feeling a shade guilty for picking so many holes in the world, he rushes to the extreme and begins to fill a few in. We can grizzle away as much as we like, he seems to say, but for heaven's sake let us sometimes open our eyes just a little wider—and look.

While he was writing these pieces in fact, Priestley had a good deal of reason to complain. The family was moving house; the fuss of two weddings intruded on his time and sundry illnesses had to be coped with; a play failed badly, and most of his teeth were pulled out "at intervals nicely calculated to keep every nerve in my head jangling". But every now and then, as the hectic tension mounted, he would slip away to his study and add a few more sentences, capture another moment that might have fled for ever. That study at Billingham Manor, where he drifted and smoked one wet idle day in 1938 and casually gave his mind to the problems of *Rain Upon Godshill*, was high on the roof and commanded a fine view. But in the new house further west at Brook the work-room was even higher above the world; one of the Delights had always been to possess a wonderful view, a large window and a broad window-seat where he could loll and gaze by the hour at a scene that changed only with the weather and the movement of the sun. The tall pine-woods and the bottle-green eiderdown of rhododendrons descend steeply into a deep-cut valley, and an escarpment surmounted by folds of farmland and meadows, bare to the seawinds, rises on the other side. Beyond, to the left and below the white haggard features of the cliffs, stretches the sea: "full in the middle panes of my window is that flashing mirror, that blue diamond or that infinite haze, that window for the mind, which is the sea". This is a landscape containing all moods, grandly conveying all weathers. A brief glance across it suggests a sudden breathless silence that can never again be broken. "The glory my eyes have seen cannot be robbed of its yesterdays."

The yesterdays file past in *Delight*, where that old readiness to net the quick butterfly of magic finds its sweetest expression in sturdy, good-humoured, poignant footnotes to a life well spent. But if yesterday has always been at the back of Priestley's work, time's winged chariot hurrying afar, today has stood firmly at the centre, and tomorrow has waited mysteriously ahead of it. One of the virtues of Priestley's work is that he has never denied the value of the past even at the risk of turning a sentimental eye to it, never attempted to escape from the present even if his sharp criticism of it meant putting his reputation in jeopardy, and never remained unaware of the future even if taking up the challenge involved him in difficult and unpopular areas of thought. He has, of course, always pleased himself, and knowing no master has perhaps relied too heavily on that unreliable combination of an idle contemplative mind and immense physical vitality. If he had been borne away by some sustaining disciplined belief that demanded more of his spirit than the gentle spasmodic faith in human life that gives his work such broad-based tolerance, he might have spoken more consistently and with greater passion, out of a narrower and more concentrated vision. But it is never relevant to discuss what a writer might have done. We have his work. Many people will always find it awkward to their minds, giving them nothing, and they will turn impatiently away. Others will find that his writing frequently coincides with their mood and speaks to them in a voice which—and this is one of the tests of good writing—they instinctively understand but which always surprises them. To turn the expected corner but to be met with the unpredictable view is a delight that might suitably have found its place in Priestley's catalogue; it comes when we read an author who holds our affection, and perhaps it springs from a sudden warming realisation that we have been shown something of what we are, how we think, the way our minds and spirits work. A writer with whom one has nothing in common, however imaginative, however deeply his eyes penetrate beneath the surface of life, has the dryness and insignificance of a text-book; we will learn nothing here, except a few facts that are probably useless.

III. An Essayist and Critic

HINTS AND GUESSES

IN 1950 I went up to Oxford and when in my second year I found myself reading a good deal of Arnold Bennett, I came across in Blackwell's a book called *Figures in Modern Literature* which Priestley wrote in 1924, shortly after he himself came down from Cambridge. Most of the essays on individual writers which compose this book appeared in the *London Mercury* and the subjects were chosen because they had not been treated at any length before. Much has now been written about most of them—about Bennett, A. E. Housman, W. W. Jacobs, Walter de la Mare—and the book therefore gave one an opportunity of assessing the worth and originality of Priestley's critical reaction to his older contemporaries. I was surprised by the book and thought it odd that Priestley should have written it. but at that time I was not aware of the way his first years of writing seemed to live a quiet life of their own behind the fat noisy novels that came later and deafened them. "Mr. Priestley is a scholar," wrote the *Morning Post*, "but he is first and foremost a critic." If that were written now, quick-tempered people of literary discrimination might well cancel their subscription to the newspaper. Then, however, it was true.

I cannot imagine Priestley attending lectures, listening with care to the dry crisp expositions of a supervisor, reading to weigh and place a book as much as to enjoy it, but the fact remains that he took a Cambridge degree in English literature and for some years afterwards followed the direction in which it logically pointed. In his later work he does not often refer to Cambridge: in *Delight* he mentions only the blossom there, the foaming branches; and he confesses in *English Journey* to the longing he always felt to "escape from King's Parade and the

Trumpington Road. I was always faintly uncomfortable, being compelled to feel—and quite rightly too—a bit of a lout and a bit of a mountebank." Nonetheless, almost everything he wrote before *The Good Companions* might well have trickled gently out of a set of college rooms overlooking gardens of blossom. "I am not pleased with myself," he goes on to say, "about this discomfort of mine at Cambridge. Probably it is because they *know*, whereas I am always only guessing." This, written in 1934, has the effect of completely denying that earlier self, represented by books composed with academic taste and manners, which made Arthur Waugh describe him as a born critic.

To crack the surface of these early works is to find, not the Priestley who might have developed differently, who should have remained at Cambridge to refine his amiable reflections on books and people to the point at which, like E. M. Forster's, they hardly produced any work at all, but the Priestley who was and is so vigorously untying knots, sorting out tangles and hacking a path through the world that he must write all the time, on any subject, very fast. For a particular purpose or piece of work, he will if necessary drop part of himself, discard like a skin a quality or an aspect of temperament, batten down a known defect so that it hardly shows; then later, for another purpose, he will take it up again and polish it brightly for publication, so that although one sometimes feels the jagged edge of inconsistency cutting into his work, it applies only to details and not to his total attitude.

After all, he guesses; he does not *know*. But his guesses, though we may feel them to be wrong at times, spring from an instinct which is consistently focussed on life and a personality which is integrated. An integrated person can do almost what he likes without being untrue to himself, for his control is unconscious, a dye inseparable from the matter it colours. In a writer, this means that whatever he says, however much it contradicts what he said yesterday or will say tomorrow, will be true, for truth is not a matter of detail, but of vision. In a way a writer like D. H. Lawrence, so unbalanced that he needed always to exert control and could not expect it naturally, requires to make a much more intellectual approach to his writing than someone like Priestley. Lawrence is uneven because that intellectual grasp was never his, because his electric intensity coursed through his books only when what few disciplines and inhibitions he had were removed by inspiration. Priestley is uneven because he is careless, because to gain his good effects he must write quickly, and by writing quickly you cannot hope to be good all the time.

Earlier on, in the years after Cambridge, he was much more careful in his work, but he was so much less experienced that the tendency to hit and miss is almost the same. T. W. Graveney, a batsman whose strokes are often as graceful and gleaming as the summer Cotswolds he represents, once confessed that the bat sometimes felt like a piece of wood in his hand. It is, of course, a piece of wood; and Priestley must occasionally have felt, being a temperamental if not an inspirational writer, that all he could get on to paper were words, not prose, not a gleaming and graceful reflection of life. For that is how it seems, particularly among the early essays in the collections that began at Cambridge in 1922 and ended with *The Balconinny* in 1929. His criticism during those years comes forward more seriously and with a slower step. Thus, in speaking of Arnold Bennett, he is not only more judicial in his writing and restrained in his thought than when throwing out a few notions, for example, on cranks and eccentrics, but he also appears to be talking directly to the novelist's face and not behind his back. This is true of his two critical biographies of Peacock and Meredith; of *The English Comic Characters*, *The English Novel* and *English Humour*; and of *Figures in Modern Literature*.

But first let us talk of the essays, for it was with these that Priestley began, unless one is indelicate enough to recall a slim volume which the youthful author preferred to forget; a volume of verses entitled *The Chapman of Rhymes* and written by a second lieutenant in the Devonshire Regiment called J. B.

Priestley. It was a limited edition brought out in 1917, becoming even more limited when Priestley destroyed a number of copies after the war and nowadays so rare that one must pay twenty guineas for it. A copy is not to be found in Albany or in the Isle of Wight; it may be consulted in the British Museum by inquisitive members of the cognoscenti with too many afternoons to spare. Prose-writers often begin with poetry in their teens, and they often feel that unless they catch a printer unawares and force him to publish it, they will die before they achieve publication. Young men can never wait; and when the thick mud of the trenches was threatening them across the channel how much more urgent must that feeling have been.

I FOR ONE

At Cambridge, Priestley started to write essays, moral tales and parodies, epigrams and trifles. This was 1922; thirty years later, in 1952, nobody at a university making their first awkward scratches with a pen would have dreamed of composing an essay either to discover what they wanted to say, or to say what they had already determined, or even to learn their craft. One wrote a weekly essay for a tutor, and that was currently the only meaning of the word: conversational in tone, it would be a hurried mixture of conventional generalisations supported by quotation from reputable critics and unorthodox ones hardly supported at all; a jumble of information indiscriminately snipped out of books late at night and badly pasted together. But to write an essay for pleasure was unthinkable. It was a dead form, reminding one curiously of a time-wasting grace of the leisured classes in writing, rather like dressing for dinner alone or spending an hour at the mirror enjoying an immaculate shave. These are not, as they may seem, idle analogies; for it is in such timeless moments, when hands are thoughtlessly occupied in some habitual exercise like dressing or shaving, that the minute germ of an idea which is blown up into an essay arrives in the writer's mind.

But today we no longer have access to the state of mind in

which such useless but diverting conceptions appear in the unanchored intelligence. Our conceptions must be vast or hasty or topical; to ride the storm of the uneasy mind we are in, an idea must be sensational, it must walk on the water or fly faster than sound. A poet *manqué* does not write essays: he joins the staff of an advertising agency, where one word is an expensive item, or he talks about the films he is going to make. For prose-writers the hasty capturing of a moment of perception nowadays finds its way into a short story, since this form has developed in such a way that the obtrusive formality of a plot can be dispensed with. The virtue of the essay is that the dimensions of space and time do not exist. The author's mind is the only dimension, which means that an essay is an abstraction of life; it is thus the nearest that prose can approach to the texture and self-sufficiency of a poem, though not to its feeling—a successful essay can often be written with as little assistance from the creative impulse as an article on a topical subject or a piece of light verse would require. A good talker, delivering a monologue, can be an essayist; he is in tune with himself, but he need not be in touch with his audience. A poet, however privately his bright words seem to flow, is always addressing a god or a muse, something outside himself. An essayist, however, need only talk to himself, though like a conversationalist he is stimulated by the waiting laughter, the ready applause.

Certainly the finest essayists in English have always been egocentric. Hazlitt was unshakeable in his opinions; Lamb often gives the impression that he did not particularly wish to hear what others had to say to him. The substance of his essays, after all, was gathered chiefly when his mind was youthfully open and receptive, and they were written when he was caged within a fussy, cantankerous middle-age. Chesterton, too, was a man firmly entrenched in his views. These are among the essayists of genius. Otherwise our literature is endowed with journalists of genius who wrote essays because they happened to be the most popular periodical exercise of the time, both early in the eighteenth century with Steele and Addison, and two hundred years later when Robert Lynd was appearing every week in the *New Statesman*. Always, until now, it was possible for a man of letters to parcel his idle reflections into neat essays and sell them to a periodical. But now they must go to waste or be imagined in a different form. The pressures of our time are too unrelaxing for the essay, which is an affair of quiet words, easily deafened by the urgencies of the present.

A GROSSLY EGOTISTICAL MATTER

Priestley has written about conversation in a long essay, *Talking*, published in 1926 as one of a series entitled 'These Diversions'. To me, and no doubt to other people of my generation, the batch of subjects chosen in this series has a wistful and attractive unreality about it, as though it existed on the other side of a black line drawn across time soon after we were born. Idling, dreaming, wandering, reading, play-going: these are the topics and although I practise them fitfully, only with concentration can I distil a rich essence of pleasure from them. I have been taught, by a bitter war, by ceaseless preparation for another and by the mechanics of living among speedy machines, that much depends on split-second timing; the best education you can buy encourages constructive thinking; the panic in the air induces one to live purposefully, even though one may be entirely without purpose. I love reading above all solitary pursuits, yet months of my life can pass when I am unable to settle to a book for more than a few minutes without feeling that a more engaging hour is to be spent in the next room. If I idle and dream and wander, the guilt steals beside me and acidly whispers its warning for the future. This uneasiness is not merely the energy of youth demanding an outlet in progress. I think it is more likely to be a refusal to believe that progress is what happens when you leave time alone and stop harrying it neurotically. It takes some time to discover one's natural tempo and it is easy to lose it again. A fast and electric civilisation like ours somewhat resembles a brass band pounding out its noisy rhythms above a serene and slowly progressive symphony. Only occasionally does the music come softly through—and even then, for some reason, it sounds guilty.

I recall reading *Talking* when spending a week-end with some friends at Cumnor, just outside Oxford, a week-end during term. At the beginning of the essay he says that "we might estimate the quality of an age by the way in which it contrives to touch with grace the common pattern of our life, exalting the crude necessities into material for art", and one of the threads he pursues, rather sadly as though he realised that talking was widely degenerating into a mere exchange of words between uncommunicating people, is the wise and gentle process of civilisation which is to be found in good talk, "as if time had rushed by for ever and we were already at ease in eternity". Once or twice, in parentheses, Priestley takes himself to task for "the almost inhuman solemnity" with which he is writing, but although in a general discursive essay of this kind an author is bound to cover a good deal of obvious ground before he can reach the subtleties of the landscape, he does explore in addition the more debatable and therefore more interesting areas.

He touches, for example, on the comedy of people unable to communicate with one another and hopelessly following different threads; and yet the heart-breaking tragedy of it. He draws attention to that thick unbreakable silence which often follows a burst of good talk, a silence which is "the very soul of irony", and which a genuinely philosophic mind can enjoy. These are the moments when Priestley approaches close to the essence of his theme, when the gestures as broad as horizons and the great sweeps of rhetoric are behind him, and his mind narrows to a single point of penetration. Apart from their worth as observations, they are valuable in the structure of the piece, for they provide that variation of pace and depth which is characteristic of Priestley's technique.

One feels that Priestley, never a consciously "fine" writer, must have seen this essay as an opportunity for fine writing, simply because the thought and construction presented no problems that could not be sorted out in half an hour's jotting on a sheet of paper. If so, it was a mistake. There is too much exuberance of phrase, a lack of discipline in the fancy which takes the sentences soaring into a rather graceless showing-off of rhetorical aerobatics. When I turned out the light in Cumnor, it was the mood and texture of the prose which had disturbed my mind, often to anger, in that malevolent condition touched off by fatigue. In the morning, however, the memory of the writing flaked away and the implications of the essay became clear. One's reaction is often thus, to an interesting writer who has still not quite mastered his manner; it is like a girl's beauty which comes through despite the clumsy way she moves and her annoying tendency to sniff. I resolved to read those earlier essays and discover how they fitted the pattern.

The essay is usually just an exercise for the wit or the fancy, and it need therefore make no attempt either to observe the truth or to approach it more closely; it is written in the first place as a brief entertainment to please the readers of some journal, and secondly, if its literary merit does not fade and curl at the edges within the week, it is collected with others into a volume. Sometimes it may represent an intense moment of revelation, in thought or feeling, but it is difficult for its effect not to be casual: life must have its footnotes which toy with one aspect of one very minor situation. These footnotes may be, like Gibbon's, almost as important and certainly as entertaining as the text; none the less one cannot help regarding them as an interruption, a moment of standing still and glancing round for the attractive anecdote or flick of wit. Once, with Bacon, it was the sermon, the sober vehicle of a thought intensely serious. Now, when fluency has succeeded urgency of thought in the curious history of our culture, and the weight of thinking per word in our literature seems to have grown steadily lighter, the essay which once crept exploratively over the beds of oceans has bobbed to the surface and there, like conversation, its "freedom to wander is of the essence of the matter". An article does not enjoy this freedom; it must stick grimly to the

point, develop it logically and bring its arguments to a persuasive conclusion. But an essay has only the logic of its wit and,
more like life, it can afford to be histrionic, unexpected, unfair
in its arguments without losing its conviction; it can twist
truth as much as it wants, provided the personality of the writer
remains steadily poised on its own odd, capricious, inexplicable axis of simply being human. For it is the most personal
form.

Although one man's essays are facets of an entire personality,
they may also be regarded as each one a personality, briefly
encountered, listened to and judged as a man might be judged
at a first meeting. When you come across him again on the
same page next week, he is someone else, playing a different
part but still, within the essay, true to himself and hence real.
The trouble I found with *Talking* was that it moved uncertainly
half-way between a lecture that had been carefully prepared
and an essay rushed off at too great a speed. Men of letters
have no right to assume that they are standing on a soapbox
when writing. The platform manner must be rigidly eschewed,
and one feels that Priestley, too slack and ranging here, doing
the job so quickly that he gives too much explanation and
emphasis to points that do not require it, has slipped into this
brow-beating way, a manner which suggests that the reader
needs to be helped into understanding as though it were a
sort of invalid chair. But the fault is a good one, for it presupposes virtues: a high regard for clarity of expression, an
informal style which is yet capable of rising to a certain full-
blooded nobility of phrase without seeming forced, and in the
interests of literature rather than of the self, a desire for the
exposure, cleanly and honestly and in the round, of the author's
own personality.

This last may not sound notably virtuous, but I have often
felt that the difficulty of conveying oneself on paper, pleasantly
and without falsehood, is something a writer must conquer
before his images of other people can satisfactorily pass that
way. Self-knowledge and self-control sharpen the wits of the
observer, while they improve his tenderness and sympathy; it

is hard work to become totally aware of one's own profound humanness, and until one has stopped being embarrassed by it, self-conscious in the choice of words to suggest it, one is unlikely to strike so deep into the heart and mind of another. A blush and a trembling hand do not become an artist.

AN IDLE SPECULATION

To prove what I thought might be the point, I made a tour of the bookshops. From the long alleys stretching towards the back of Blackwell's, came a copy of *Papers from Lilliput*, which Bowes and Bowes published in Cambridge in 1922. It is a selection of essays contributed to various London literary journals, the *Cambridge Review* and the *Yorkshire Observer*. But of *I For One*, brought out in the following year by John Lane, there was no sign, and I was forced to take steps that were at that time much against my principles. Without cigarettes, my head heavy with the stupor of time hanging fire, I spent an afternoon in the suppressed racket of a library, now and then raising my eyes to the arid spectacle of pursed lips, chewed pencils and girls gently sweating at the eyebrows. But reading a book of essays from cover to cover resembles the impossible task of digesting a thirty-course meal; trailing thankfully to the end of the tenth essay, one finds the eleventh pushed brightly in front of one, requiring a brisk renewal of an already satiated interest. You cannot read thirty essays in a row and hope to be affected by them as the author intended; they are occasional pieces and should therefore be read occasionally.

In the early essays of Priestley contained in the two books I found at Oxford, the young man postures excessively as if unsure of his audience; he has not yet learned—though he quotes Goethe as saying it—to write with a million readers in view, or alternatively he has so far never discovered the trick of not caring a rap for his readers. "The audience is huge," he says in "Audacity in Authorship", "it plays the part of a vast, drowsy auctioneer lolling above a clamouring crowd of buyers,

men-of-letters trying to catch its eye; and what avail now are
the level tones and the sober argument when only a squeak or
a roar or an insane gesture is likely to attract attention?"
Here is one of the roars; and another loudly breaks the silence
in "Those Terrible Novelists", a piece of somewhat heavy-
handed irony which again seems uncertain of its reception and
appears therefore as a gauche and insincere attack on the
"serious, intellectual, satirical" novels which make the reader
long "to escape into the clean open air of a genuine tale". It
is true that such novels (the work of Aldous Huxley, for
example) do not accord with Priestley's view of fiction or, and
this does not necessarily follow, give him much pleasure as a
reader. But his true critical reaction is not reflected in this total
and insensitive failure to comprehend them. He is writing down
to the imagined audience, that vast and drowsy auctioneer, and
he is waiting with an ear half-cocked for its ignorant good-
hearted applause. Thus at one moment he is siding massively
with the forces of complacent intolerance and doing literature
a disservice for the sake of an attitude; at the next, in "An
Idle Speculation", by wondering what would happen if the
national interest in football suddenly swung round to books,
long queues forming outside the libraries and four pages of
reviews in all the dailies, he is sharply complaining of the
blank face which people turn to the world of books. One does
not expect consistency in any writer. But this is not inconsistency of viewpoint; it is a failure to make consistent contact
with the nature of the audience no less than with the character
of oneself. Unsure of the company they are keeping, these
essays never entirely relax.

Yet even as early as this, taking a rush at the barriers of self-
consciousness and getting somewhat entangled in them, the
personalities both true and produced of the author show clearly
through the kind of subject that touches him and the reflections
it prompts. One week Priestley awoke from an afternoon dream
and almost breathlessly he sat down and described it, noting the
wonder of dreams, the complexity of something which "makes
even literature seem little more than its attenuated, halting

shadow". Later, dreams would never be far from the troubled nights of his characters and there are times when his work, even on the stage, takes on the evanescent and illogical beauty of a dream. And from dreams he is constantly returning to that "land of Heart's Desire, only to be found on maps of moonshine", which even found its way into the title of his first novel. When as a boy he took his weekly penny and stared for an hour into the sweet-shop window, he invariably chose that unknown quantity, the Lucky Bag, and always he was disappointed; you cannot have the land of Heart's Desire for a penny. You never get something for nothing either, but there is still a little poetry left in the belief that you can. Praising the Eternal Cheap Jack who opens his attaché case at street-corners or gathers an open-mouthed crowd in the markets, Priestley comes back to this dream, this sad but not disheartened glance over the shoulder to the regions where we are still children: "when we have entirely forsaken the idea, then we are lost indeed, for it comes from the depths of our primal innocence, and has about it the last lingering scent of the Garden of Eden."

The fleeting, the vanished, the thin as gauze, the liable to disappear at a touch, this insubstantial pageant as one of these essays is called: these are the moments to be tracked and captured, to last an essay through, to discover something of the world and a little more of oneself.

Time and again in these first collections it is as though Priestley were tune-haunted. "It is curious that music," he says, "once it has filtered into the memory, should always lose any gaiety it might have once had and turn regretful, softly hymning a world of lost endeavour." When conjuring with the image of an old conjuror or recalling incredulously three strange quiet men who lived and died in a small town or running across a mad shepherd who guided his imaginary sheep through the streets, he seems to be deliberately playing, not for laughs but for tears, to be regretting, not the past but the poetry he ought to have written in his youth. His eyes are not quite focussed on the world, and he still cannot accurately listen to the beating of his own heart and hear the words it murmurs. Fluency and wit present a smooth surface, but the undercurrents are quixotic, unreliable, a dangerous sphere of half-emotions struggling for full breath. It seems in these early essays that the light has turned golden and diaphanous before its time, that autumn has been called into play more as a stage property than a true season. Later in Priestley's work this sweet melancholy will assume the much subtler tones of reality. For the moment it is sweeter than honeysuckle, too sweet. Some of these boyish impulses, perhaps, never grow up in Priestley's work—his humour, for example, occasionally strikes people as a still childish attempt to throw off the burden of reality—but this one remains, maturing, finding its strength in the quiet distillation of experience, reaching its full power in *Bright Day* and *The Linden Tree.*

Literally these are essays; Priestley is trying his hand. What sort of writer is he? No one knows. He is finding out: at one moment taking tight little steps like a skater with his hand on the rail, at the next plunging awkwardly forward, all legs, shouting at the top of his voice. On several occasions the true balance is struck, and almost without realising it I found I had read an essay that stuck in the mind, buds of phrases which blossomed and stayed fresh for a week. I recalled the social tortures of dealing with a hostess who insisted on calling him Mr. Barker, his inability to sleep at night and his longing to doze off during the day; I sat next to him in railway compartments sharing his vivid intolerant reactions to the other travellers, and I accompanied him when he tried to buy some cheap socks at an outfitter's shop; I too waited anxiously for the postman to bring the fabulous letter that is always expected but never comes; and when he suddenly began to describe a journey through London at dusk on the top of a bus and brought to the task such a clean and unusual perception of beauty, I suffered an agonising response, a feeling that I had been fatuously blind to these wonders for years. For even in those early days Priestley was concerned with indicating sources of wonder.

But if we cannot yet tell for certain what sort of writer he is, we at least discover something of the man. He plays the piano badly, he is inquisitive and dogmatic, he is fond of cards and music and walking, but hates strangers and filling in forms; he has no objection to mummer-worship and believes that exaggeration is one of art's greatest devices. His mind does nothing but wander aimlessly, for he is of a discursive habit with strong but eccentric powers of association; and then again, his first impressions are generally wrong, and though he is ready to argue from them, he distrusts them so much that he would never act upon them. Here and there glimpses appear, but the skeleton is not yet inimitably clothed with flesh. A man still feeling his way might turn out to be anyone; Priestley has still to face his readers brazenly, to announce that the gates are open and the undergrowth cleared. This is the point which authors always reach; Lawrence arrived as soon as he had written *The Plumed Serpent*; it was the reason why Virginia Woolf forbade any novelist to publish before he was thirty. Priestley is not there but the signs are, and books are worth reading for their signs, particularly when they were not intended as signs at all but as part of a fluid intermittent design in which a young and developing writer was steadily trying to feel at home. These signs, however, glow and twinkle like stars, and we should follow them like wise men.

A SHARPENING OF THE PENCIL

I delayed such wisdom while still at Oxford for I followed those signs only hesitantly, reading an occasional essay when I came across it but spending more time in searching for passages in Priestley's criticism which I could pretend (though this was not always necessary) would be of help to me in my work. But I did not know that after *I For One* in 1923 Priestley published no more essays for four years, and then three volumes appeared at yearly intervals, *Open House* in 1927, *Apes and Angels* in 1928 and *The Balconinny* in the same year as *The Good Companions*. Even I, picking up these later essays briefly when passing a guilty hour in bookshops where I intended to spend no money, could hardly fail to discern the difference which the intermission had made to his work of this kind. It was as though he had spent those years in learning, by means of more objective writing, a good deal about himself that was tentative, smudgy, almost apologetic in the earlier pieces. Eric Gillett has suggested that the essays contained in these three volumes may be ranged alongside Max Beerbohm's as the finest of this century. The last hints of Lamb and Stevenson—even their names cropped up frequently in the first collections—have disappeared, most of the literary references have been dispensed with, as if Priestley knew that he could now with confidence stand on his own feet, and the phrases are no longer obviously turned for effect. The respectable lace-curtains of traditions and influences have been torn out of the essayist's window, and Priestley is standing there firmly, not only commanding a much clearer view of the scene beyond the window but also offering a brighter, more honest and disarmingly vulnerable picture of himself. Many of the themes which picked their way too delicately through the earlier pieces—the glimpses of magic, the dreams, the eccentric byways—are still in evidence, but they have become adult, they stand poised above the precipice of dying falls but never drop, they stride through the purple landscapes of rhetoric but never pause for long. The irony now quietly penetrates its object like a hypodermic needle and spreads the essence through its veins.

The total success of these essays, of which I still often find a volume on my bedside table, seems to lie in the fact that Priestley no longer cares about a number of matters which once awkwardly obsessed him: he has relaxed into writing idly, letting the words look after themselves and concentrating only on the way his whole mind and personality is put at the service of the subject. If words are repeated in adjacent sentences or a way of stating something clearly lacks any deliberate music, it does not matter, for the value of words now resides, not in any handsome pattern they might make but in what they will say as quickly and cleanly as possible. If admittedly they are called upon for a passage of description, as in "First Snow", then their value is considered more carefully. A natural writer of prose can only approach poetry by stringing words of colour, weight and atmosphere along the threads of his sentences, subtly spaced like magic lanterns, for the reading mind is not fitted to take prose sentences in which every word has been weighed on the same delicate scales as a poet would use; prose poems are usually unreadable. But in general Priestley's style becomes in these essays what it has always remained, an instrument so unconsciously tuned to whatever its owner wishes to say, so lacking in calculation, that it reveals the personality behind it as fully and naturally as if he were talking in the calmest of companies.

There are no shadows now, no stage-fright. The lights have been switched on full, and though Priestley occupies the centre of the stage, he does so only to make quite certain that we are clearly hearing the lines he speaks and are noticing such details of the constantly shifting scenery as he is concerned to point out. He neither whispers nor bullies, but between these extremes his voice is capable of much variety, his face is as expressive and consistent as a character actor's, and his observations lead us to contemplate every aspect of the back-cloth which a flick of the fingers has brought down from the flies, even those aspects which are invisible to the naked eye. An extended theatrical metaphor is not without point: although Priestley had given no sign at the time these essays were written that he would turn to the drama, his interest in the subject frequently appears in a choice of topic (like "First Nights" or "Our Theatre") or in a casual aside. One always likes to recognise an attitude or identify an image in the earlier works of an author because these are the lines of communication between past and present, the threads that give his work consistent direction as well as an odd human frailty in his repetitions.

Priestley often repeats himself or employs his material again in only a slightly different form, and when he is obsessed with a point—often in answer to critics of his work—these repetitions can be very galling to his admirers. It is none the less interesting when some reference or description in the essays sets up an echo in the mind which can be identified as a link with one of the later books, and this is often happening. In "The Inn of the Six Anglers", Priestley recounts a wet storm-swept journey through Wales looking for somewhere to spend the night, and I was at once carried forward to *Benighted* which must have been written not long after this essay and which doubtless occurred to his mind as he peered through the windscreen of his car that bleak night. The Thorlaws in "Open House", although they lack the sophistication of the Alington family in *Bright Day*, belong to the same world; for both Priestley and Gregory Dawson these familes are "dimly consecrated in my memory by a happiness that something seems to have withered away, shining there in a queer kind of Golden Age". And also, in an essay called "T'Match", we find the leisurely opening sequence of *The Good Companions*, even to the grey-green tide of cloth caps that can be seen emerging sluggishly from the football ground at Bruddersford.

But there are not only these direct links between the essays and the later fiction. Since Priestley as a good journalist tends to exploit the immediacy of his experience as well as subsequently its deeper effect on him, we are often introduced to the atmosphere and circumstances of his life at times when he was engaged in the writing of his books. In *The Balconinny*, for example, he finely describes the prospect of the sea towards Goodwin Sands which he would watch morning and evening from his house on the coast, and as this essay appeared in the *Saturday Review* in 1928, these paragraphs may obviously be taken as a marginal note of biography referring to that summer which Priestley spent with his family at Wardley, The Marina, Deal, where he was writing *The Good Companions*—and thus again we are plunged into the man's life. Most of the essays in these volumes are shaped to fit into a jigsaw of Priestley's movements during the later twenties, to indicate the outward appearance of his days as well as the pressures and concerns of his mind, and although there would be pieces missing, an

astute and patient biographer could no doubt provide a
reasonably true picture of where and how and in what state of
mind his subject's time was spent. Apart perhaps from the two
"chapters" of autobiography written towards the end of the
thirties, we can never learn so directly what Priestley is like
anywhere else in his work. He was well over thirty when these
essays appeared and if some of his attitudes have changed
since then, the basic personality which set those attitudes on
their feet had hardened (or perhaps softened is a truer word)
into maturity sufficiently to produce, quite soon, some of his
best creative work.

Honesty and plain speaking, however cynical we sometimes
are at their expense, are attractive qualities, and when their
sharp edges are planed away by a half-humorous tenderness, a
pastel affection for the physical world and for the antics of men,
a combination is created which gently lulls and enchants the
senses at the same time as it buffets and stimulates the mind.
We must not expect too much; these are still footnotes. Only
later is Priestley at pains to grab hold of us roughly by the arm
and force us to accept an aspect of the world as he sees it. With
a mild comment or a sudden excitement, he is strolling across
the lawns and through the rose-tangles of a private place,
which we are at liberty to share if we wish. An example of this
occurs in "A Fish in Bayswater". He is wandering down a
street out of spirits, the victim of a mood in which "life had
seemed no better than the stirring of withered leaves against
a grey wall"; and he sees on a fishmonger's slab a very large
flat fish. He halted, and his mind was instantaneously filled
with a vision of the sea.

Here he describes the total momentary presence of an object,
the full vision that comes only to men who are drowning; a
moment of ecstasy in our lives, making the present a heady
amalgam of the past and cutting out the future altogether,
must be very like going under for the last time. "This was, you
see, no common glimpse, a peep through the misty spectacles
of custom, but a sudden flashing vision, a brief acquaintance
with what we might call the thing-in-itself, even though it was

tangled with all manner of personal associations and memories."
An essay seems to have happened by chance, and it is in stumbling across such moments, a curtain being briefly drawn aside
by an unseen hand, a sky clearing of clouds for a minute, that
Priestley excels. Sometimes they are trivial and we smile and
pass on: the mind finds a curious satisfaction in a fuss made
out of nothing. "There are occasions in a man's existence when
he must make something happen, must fling a splash of colour
into his life, or some part of him, perhaps the boy in him, will
perish, flying broken before the grey armies of age, timidity or
boredom." The subject here is a pair of crimson silk pyjamas
which Priestley bought one wet morning in a Bond Street
shop; witty, excited, rather grand, the words pursue an un-
important moment, a marginal glimpse of reality, that we
should be poorer without.

But sometimes, too, the stakes are higher, the mood is
heightened and the effect is breath-taking. The prose rambles
on reflectively, and quite suddenly into it strikes the loud
resonant note of the experience, half out of this world but
momentarily forcing the world into a stranger pattern. There
is the simple but terrifying vision of "The Tiger" that occurred
to him as he sat behind the chauffeur in a silent wealthy car;
"the tiger did not spring, so I am still alive. But I caught the
gleam of an eye, a whiff of hot, rank breath." There is that
desperate tragic vision that came to him in a bus as he jour-
neyed down the desolate length of Haymarket, "as if a huge
black stone had been flung into the pool of my consciousness".
And, in "Seeing Stratford", a warmer and gentler climate of
mood brings forth one of those glimpses like a flower, a rosy
unsentimental vision of the people from Shakespeare who
might have walked that way, a stroke of the spring sunlight.
Already the sweet melancholy of those earlier essays has found
its lovely, actual autumn, and the same mood inspires and
pervades much of the human sympathetic criticism to be found
in *The English Comic Characters*.

TO THE GOLDEN AGE

In my last year at Oxford I read an essay of Priestley's called "Thick Notebooks" in which he describes how, when killing time in the Broad, he caught sight of a pile of these notebooks displayed in the windows of several booksellers and how his mind turned to the stuffy high-pitched tedium of tutorials, the drab traipse to the examination rooms "on the very rose-crowned threshold of June". The endless taking of notes: how solemn, how idiotic, and how I agreed with him. My own thick notebooks were never broached further than a limp page or two of words I would never read again, helpless quotations which, out of context, I could never subsequently understand. These chapters on Priestley might have been very different if I had been addicted at Oxford to thick notebooks. But I preferred instead—and who does not?—to walk across the Broad away from the windows of notebooks and perhaps into the gardens of Trinity, where I remember one summer afternoon, too close for safety to the panic of the examinations, reading Hemingway's *Fiesta* under a tree; once or twice the falling petals drifted over the page in a sensuous indulgent fashion that Hemingway might have regretted. I wish, though, that I had taken a volume of Priestley's criticism with me into those gardens, for ever since reading *The English Comic Characters* I have associated it with afternoons, which do not end but glide imperceptibly into another condition of time; in mornings and evenings the clock ticks and every minute changes, but in the afternoons, as in sleep, one is not aware of it and that is the time for reading.

With a shameless view to snipping out quotations and possibly inscribing them in a thick notebook, I read the chapters in *The English Comic Characters* which are concerned with Shakespeare: on Bottom, Touchstone, the comedy figures in *Twelfth Night* and of course on Falstaff. They did not, however, help me much. In this book, as in *English Humour*, Priestley's method is not so much to throw out a challenging series of critical generalisations and then astutely to pull them in again by means of a close study of the text, emerging satisfactorily at the end of the process with a cast-iron case; he reserves that more detailed and disciplined method for the formal biographies of Meredith and Peacock. His purpose here is to evoke, almost as though he were creating the characters himself, finding his material for the task in the inspiration of the plays rather than in the imaginative recesses of his own mind. He is not really assuming a critical mantle at all, but throwing off his cloak and settling down by the fire as an entertainer, a story-teller, delving in our common memories for his subject-matter and hoping through the light he casts on it and the atmosphere he conveys for it to render it freshly, with greater clarity, with his own excitement. It was obviously a book he loved the thought of writing, and there is consequently more warm enthusiasm than cold analysis in its pages. All useful criticism, however crisp and unrelaxing its martial parade of words may seem, springs from an intense warmth of interest and a desire to share precisely and in mental terms an appreciation of the heart. But Priestley is only sympathetic where the things he likes are concerned. No impatient man can unearth a critical system which will allow every type of writer to have a place in it. This is one of the few defences for critics who are not themselves practitioners of the art they serve, not only that their literary sympathies cover a wider field but that wherever they stand in that field they can dig deeper wells of understanding. A creative writer should not possess a fair mind or be understanding to the last inch of the world, for the lack of an attitude weakens his impact.

This is not to suggest that Priestley's sympathies are narrow or his understanding superficial, but it is always possible to detect in his criticism those moments of uneasy perception or uncertain view which are the mark of the amateur, the man who loves books too hungrily to keep quiet across difficult territory. It is in my opinion no defect, for anything that is said about a book by an intelligent man is worth hearing, and if his feelings concentrate on a certain sphere of literature because they are naturally at home there, the conclusions he reaches about that sphere will be intense in their feeling and perhaps unique in their value. With Priestley this area of particular sympathy covers the whole of comedy, and specifically English comedy. I doubt if any critic has recorded such an attuned and spontaneous reaction to the various expressions, in Shakespeare, Dickens, Sterne, Jane Austen and Fielding, of the spirit of English comedy, and certainly none has written about it with such immediacy, as though the ink were still damp on Falstaff's speeches and the leaves in the Forest of Arden had still to fall. This great advantage the amateur has over the professional: he is not called upon to persuade or instruct, since he is merely airing a hobby, sharing a pleasure with those in whom his terms of reference strike an answering chord. Both in *English Humour* and *The English Comic Characters* the gentle humours of the writing and the subtle reconstruction of the characters have more in common with the natural springs of fiction than with the deep critical reservoirs; the quick crystal water flows until it deepens gradually into a river, instead of merely possessing that still motionless depth in which the valuable conclusions of didactic or analytical criticism are drawn.

THE GENTLE CRITIC SMILES

Priestley's first book, *Brief Diversions*, published at Cambridge in 1922, contains a litter of small pieces of varying kinds, for the most part those contrived knick-knacks of artifice and wit which are both as graceful and as ubiquitous as the etchings popular at that time: outlandish moral tales, donnish and quaint, that have the feeling of a motto in a rather superior cracker; a handful of epigrams which emphasise a point Priestley makes elsewhere, in his essay on A. E. Housman, that English is not a language that naturally clicks into epigrammatic form; but finally, by far the most impressive, a collection of parodies so good that one is involved, not in that satisfied smile that usually attends effective parodies, but in giving attention to what might easily be a new work by the authors parodied. They are, if anything, too good, and thus indirectly they establish Priestley as the kind of critic who is not concerned with estimating an author's performance and tearing him inside out to reveal the sources, structures and tensions of his work, but with the happy chance of finding himself, as an articulate individual, so close to the living essence of a work that he is too excited to keep quiet about it. In the parodies he became so closely identified with the spirit of Yeats, de la Mare, Housman, that for a brief moment he held their pens for them, and the same proximity is the secret of his criticism. One may be too near to make a reasoned assessment of value, but one cannot be near enough to comprehend the essence of a work.

In the evocations of the comic characters Priestley's prose takes on a glowing internal warmth which gives it a kind of grace unusual in his writing, a heightened ability to make poetical effects of some delicacy. There is no doubt that the subject matter is responsible for this, for Priestley finds a deeper and more touching expression of poetry in the comic vision than in the tragic; it is that fact which has caused others to describe him as a "near-poet", one whose heart hammers faster at the spectacle of life rather than occasionally misses a beat. Melancholy, not tragedy, appeals to him; it enters frequently and with an incalculable power to touch the reader into his work; and it is a quality which lies at the root of the comic vision and lends it a significance no less profound than the more obvious power of tragedy.

In *George Meredith*, a crisp and masterly piece of analytical criticism which clarifies an awkward subject with an insight that Meredith does not normally inspire, Priestley wriggled still further into the intricacies of the comic genius, and the chapter which precedes a detailed discussion of the novels is an object lesson in lucid exposition. This volume, which appeared in 1926 and was written under extreme pressure when his wife was dying of cancer, is a work both more difficult and more devoted than his *Thomas Love Peacock* which came out in the following year. One suspects an ability, which is characteristic of Priestley's type of mind, to rise to a challenging occasion much more successfully if the challenge seems beyond his powers. Peacock, although his matter is rich in opportunities for critical discussion, remains a simple and consistent writer, requiring much less interpretation than Meredith. For one thing, he is far enough away from us to be judged in the perspective of his time, whereas Meredith's concerns are still urgent, his age still shouts confusingly at the back of us and his idiom resists measurement by the conventional Victorian yardstick that we might reasonably apply to George Eliot or even to Hardy.

By these problems Priestley is never defeated. With Meredith it was essential to stand away from the subject so as to see it at all, and in casting the general glance that such a method necessitates Priestley managed to glimpse all the details that were crucial to a portrait of a man, a summary of his thought and an appreciation of his creative work. The crispness of the writing, occasioned by a formal absence of personality courteous in such a book, allows the subject to occupy all four dimensions of the work, as though no expression of personal opinion but only a strict adherence to fact could be permitted.

In this type of criticism, which possesses only the usual dimensions and leaves no room for doubt, the mind which, acting alone, is most readily detached from temperament must be placed in full command of the operation. It would have been impertinent as well as useless to have treated a matter of such angular intellectual difficulty as Meredith in any other fashion. Character and situation, the poetry of time and event, are trivial in Meredith unless they are viewed through a mind steeped in the highly individual substance of his thought; until that has been mastered, his heart seems abnormal. Creative writing is not, like criticism, limited to four dimensions: they are innumerable, and the angles of vision needed to grasp the perspective in Meredith must be pointed out and explained. By retiring from the book altogether, by removing, as it were, the dimension of his own personality which entered so warmly into the flavour of *The English Comic Characters*, Priestley has written an exemplary introduction to Meredith, his truest work of the mind.

Figures in Modern Literature is concerned with the living, the still producing: nine writers who in 1924 were among the brightest stars in the particular firmament which Priestley favoured. The studies are all therefore somewhat tentative, interim reports, designed for the *London Mercury* to bring these authors once more into the public eye and to summarise their achievement to date. The best of them may be regarded as general prefaces to the complete works of the authors they treat, for brief though they are, Priestley indirectly contrives to draw a sketch of the man by delving into the most characteristic elements of his work. The picture of Arnold Bennett that emerges is so lively and freehand that one doubts whether even a full-length biography could have conveyed his attitude so vividly.

But irrespective of the quality of the criticism which is always at ease, adroit, even witty in its phrasing and conducted with a gentleness and patience that are invaluable qualities in a critic of modern writing, I found that much of the book's interest lay not only in this particular selection of authors but in the aspects of their production which Priestley chose, or thought himself qualified, to deal with. Once again, it is almost as though he were partly writing both for himself and about himself. Although it might be irresponsible to suggest that in these critical works he was unconsciously preparing for the plays and novels he would later write himself, he must have learned a good deal from the emphasis of his critical perceptions, and it might be said that in these various excursions into the literature of the past and present he was helped to discover what exactly he wanted to do.

One of the first points he makes about Bennett is that "he has one quality that is an essential ingredient of great romance —a sense of wonder". Yet he lacks "philosophic imagination, a quality of mind that is present, at their best, in Hardy, Meredith, Conrad . . . it is this quality that can make a scene in a farm-kitchen an affair of the Gods and the Titans and yet still a scene in a farm-kitchen". Bennet was saved from the "thin, rigid, brittle narratives" that the strong French influence might have induced him to write by a divinity that shaped his ends: the Five Towns. When such remarks are applied to the work of Priestley, they give us grounds on which to begin our search for an acceptable view of him. Again, in the felicitous essay on Walter de la Mare, after being told of a tendency to treat the poet as if he were "not an artist with a unique vision, a man of strange delights and sorrows, but a rather gentlemanly conjuror they had engaged for a children's party", we come across a passage about "an imagination of an unusual kind, one that is infinitely wider and more sensitive than a child's, and yet, in one sense, still is a child's imagination". And here once more we find ourselves neck-high in a discussion that touches Priestley's own work closely. The book's range is wide, and though it is improbable that posterity will confirm Priestley's opinion of swiftly fading writers like Maurice Hewlett and J. C. Squire, the studies of Housman, W. W. Jacobs, and George Saintsbury are not only valuable as contemporary estimates of those writers but also offer a reflection, poised and unshuddering, of Priestley's general view of the branches of art they practised: poetry, the short story, essays and criticism. Generalisation is never tacked smugly on to the subject; it is merely, for the purposes of discussion and illumination, drawn gently out of the texts under survey. Here, in the pitiable unwalked corners of libraries, lies another book of Priestley's which has been obscured by the enormous bulk of the later novels and the reputation they brought him.

But criticism has lost Priestley. A number of possibilities were put forward to publishers during the later twenties (*The Worlds of Fiction*, never written, was among them), but there were other worlds to conquer, more to his taste. Subsequently his critical writing turned into the popular quick-fire drug required by the newspapers, which serves its purpose only if it is slapdash and unreasonable; in the *Evening News* in 1928 Priestley rivalled Arnold Bennett once a week, and later succeeded him on the *Evening Standard*. Either in fact or in

E

spirit, he never again took the slow patient train to Cambridge and settled down to read in uninterrupted rooms—like those rooms he occupied for a term in the tiny lodge at the back gate of his college, described in "A Vanished Lodging". But one cannot regret those years tucked away comfortably in the twenties, with their impression of low lights, heaps of books and a half-finished essay on the table; one only regrets that readers of Priestley too rarely turn back to them. If Priestley himself had turned back, his nature would have been poorly served. When he quoted "I'll to the Cam no more, the laurels all are cut", he meant it.

IV. A Promising Young Novelist

IT was a brusque and quarrelsome November day and I took the morning express from King's Cross to Bradford. I had been invited to give a talk on a literary subject to the Bradford English Society; I chose J. B. Priestley who had once been president of the society and whose work I felt the members would be sure to know. It is always advisable to reserve a seat at King's Cross, for many people travel north at all times of the year, and while I was settling into my seat I was aware that next door, at St. Pancras, "the most canonical of all our stations" was busy with the opening sentences of *Adam in Moonshine*, the first of Priestley's novels and published in 1927.

A few years before Priestley was writing *Adam in Moonshine*, Aldous Huxley had begun his first journey into fiction in a small local train chuffing steadily towards that eccentric sphere of elegant and articulate culture which, through all his novels, carries an atmosphere no less fantastic than Priestley's more explicit excursion into fantasy. For *Adam in Moonshine*, after the careful realistic journey of its opening, turns out to be an explosion of magic, a display of fireworks which is particularly designed to celebrate the common taken-for-granted miracles of day and night. Into the first page, oddly, creeps a flavour of Aldous Huxley. Like Denis in *Crome Yellow*, Adam Stewart is given a pause for reflection as he makes the fussy pensive preparations for his long journey to the north, his adventure. "The locomotives grunted and wheezed like outraged sacristans. The thin high voices of the newsboys ran together into a protesting chorus of virgins and elders. But no, that was Greek drama, Adam reminded himself, and nothing to do with cathedrals. . . ." And yes, here he is, we think: not the brash shrugging young figure of the fifties who swaggers through fiction with a sneer for cultural name-dropping and a testy ignorance of ideas, but the bright boy of the twenties fed on good texts and art galleries, nourished in the suave and elegant saloons of the Italian riviera and the home counties.

This is Priestley, but it might for the moment be Huxley. One should remember that these two writers, always perhaps too far apart to be photographed together at ease in the critical garden, were none the less making their first excursions (if not sounding their first alarms) in the twenties, in the same decade. Later, in the light of subsequent development, it becomes almost ludicrous to suggest links between writers so different in both aim and achievement, but one should never deny comparisons that might once have occurred to a reader. To compare Priestley with Zola would seem a critical affectation more calculated to prove the agility of the critic than to throw light on either author. But some years ago Alan Pryce-Jones did responsibly make the comparison, and it is critically more just to Priestley, whatever the result in agreement or under-standing, to set him beside the massive uneven ranges of Zola's novels than to recall him in isolation as the author of a jolly comfortable book called *The Good Companions*.

I was pleased that *Adam in Moonshine* opened under the vault of St. Pancras, with the possibility of adventure hissing in the steam of engines and bustling among the crowds, because I had determined to read the book once more that morning when I went to King's Cross to catch the express to Bradford. Some books suit certain places: one reads Hardy in gardens below the hills, and tightlipped detectives should only light cigarettes and nod briefly on sleepless nights. Priestley's first novel begins at a London terminus, closes in a remote country waiting-room and should be read, not too quickly, on a journey. Writers set their own speed of reading and depend on the reader's co-operation for their effects: the slow mustering of tragedy in Thomas Hardy dumbly retreats like an idiot yokel if you race through his novels, his prose is rugged and the span of the action seems tilted upward as though to force the reader to make a gentle climb of it. But usually, in Priestley, you must run before you can walk, rush hurriedly over the ground before stopping to consider at leisure the various points of interest that have caught your eye. He is not a careful writer in the most refined sense, and would lose much of his sweep and immediacy if he laboured at his page; the reader, therefore, should never pause too long for dissection and analysis.

Priestley's subtlety does not lie in the patterning of words, the construction of sentences deliberately to open fresh and originally slanted windows on his subject matter, the delicate modelling of phrases. He achieves instead, in his best work, a colloquial directness of communication between himself and his reader which can almost make it appear that the writer is avoiding the use of words altogether. As with oysters, the savour is in the swallowing. The idea, the atmosphere, the character, are gone before you can catch them. If a writer has something worth saying, he must determine whether he will convey the experience by the effacement of language like Graham Greene, the surface of whose prose is so concrete and unimagined that the reader's sense of reality and not his fancy is enchained, or by the removal of attitude which even Flaubert at the extreme could never perfect, or by the abundant and powerful persuasions of style like Conrad or Henry James. Priestley does not discourage fancy, but his flights into imagery often let you down with a bump because the simple and uninvolved fluency of his style have led you to expect, quite rightly, that naturalism is basic to his vision. He has, so to speak, effaced language and substituted personality, which leads him to use with a loose conversational relish big gesticulating images and adjectives of vast exaggeration. "Vast" happens to be one of them; and I am doubtless exaggerating. At all events these faults appear later, hardly at all in *Adam in Moonshine*.

These points about Priestley's manner should be emphasised, for they help to explain why I believed I should learn more about his work by travelling to Bradford one morning in November than by taking pages of studious notes and annotating margins in the British Museum; why, in fact, I am jotting down what comes into my head about Priestley rather than quoting, analysing, conjecturing, penetrating, exposing, and trying to reveal in the higher reaches of criticism a talent I do not possess. I come to Priestley as one who, presented with an unavoidable journey or an evening free of engagements, opens a book and reads; who runs his eye along a library shelf and selects a volume because it seems at that moment to meet the case; who lies in bed at night with the light burning half an hour too long; who reads because there is pleasure there; who handles books because he cannot help it.

When a human being, subject to a constantly changing depth of mood, a veering of attitude, an alteration of his needs and demands on life, turns to a world of such variety as books offer, he cannot rigidly maintain critical standards, either high or low, without making a narrow generalisation of his own personality. People of catholic taste in art are often those to whom no art, even the failed or the grotesquely out of fashion, is in bad taste, and I believe catholicity is much to be desired in reading; there is much in a human being that fails or is out of fashion or in bad taste, and giving our tastes full rein, without imposing a restrictive set of values on them, keeps us sparklingly aware of the ramifications of being alive. This is not to suggest that in reading we should lack the ability to distinguish and define; indeed it is to stress the value of that ability at the expense of judgment according to principles. We do not finally judge; we read, we think and we talk.

I did not talk on my journey northwards through the Midlands, nor did I think. I was reading *Adam in Moonshine*, perhaps too fast. For it is one of the few novels of Priestley's in the writing of which an almost self-conscious care appears to have been exercised. One suspects that birth was slower and more painful than with the much bigger bouncing babies that were shortly to follow it. The reason for this, perhaps, is not that Priestley was touched by a first novelist's awareness that he was delicately coming to grips with the divine sources of art (he was already too old a hand to be patient with such attitudes), but quite simply that his particular purpose here required a delicacy, a dancing music in the words which would reconcile a series of absurd and fantastic events with the outward world of reality which we often, selfishly or in bad moods, find so drab. The book designs to make us sit up and take notice, not to make magic but to point it out.

This has always been a concern of Priestley's: sometimes he forces on his readers the tonic of unlikely occurrences or behaviour, to excite their perception of the real world and make it lively once again; sometimes he explicitly comes forward in the figure of J. B. Priestley, as he does with such unaffected feeling in *Delight*, to indicate certain pleasures the world offers, which we in our fuss and hurry might be missing. *Adam in Moonshine*, rather than setting out to open magic casements and produce the faery lands with a flick of the wand, is lightly trying to show that every window is a casement and all seas are perilous.

Priestley, something of a showman, is always juggling close to the edge of the stage, and we often hold our breath in the fear that a sudden lapse will send a club or a coloured ball crashing into the footlights. In the theatre he has hurled the dimension of time into the air like a challenge, and most often it has been accepted with applause. His first novel, without sophistication or the restraint that keeps a writer safe and remote from unfavourable criticism behind his private curtain, belongs to the territory, full of potholes and unexpected quicksands, where poets find their feet; it is the territory close to the edge of failure, and you can remain balanced there only by playing tremendously safe or by throwing in your imagination with total courage. This is what Priestley did with *Adam in Moonshine*. He is fanciful, melodramatic, romantic, youthful, idiotic; he is naïve, sincere, a shade clumsy, wonderfully foolish, and he rushes into poetic moments as though determined to crush them for ever. "She was standing there in the middle of the room, a finger at her lip. The closely curtained place with its single candle flame, dim, warm, faintly scented, was her casket. She seemed smaller and slighter and yet more rounded than before, seemed to shine through her loose green

wrap, as she stood there lifting to him eyes and lips that had
borrowed some touch of darkness from the surrounding dusk."
Even in 1927 no one could seriously hope to write like this, and
get away with it. E. M. Forster had finished with the novel
and was drifting in carpet slippers through his gentle rooms,
Aldous Huxley was spreading along the fashionable shelves,
Katherine Mansfield had written and would write no more,
and D. H. Lawrence had little left to achieve beyond that cut
of the censor's lash that would hold Lady Chatterley at bay
for more than a quarter of a century. Yet Priestley, held at that
time within the same atmosphere of regard as such writers as
these, merely for the promise he had shown as a critic and
essayist, achieved success in this book because, however over-
fancied his sentences might sound out of context, the balance
within the work between realism and fantasy was maintained
by the strict discipline he had learned in fields more demanding than fiction. Literary journalism shapes the craftsman
well.

   The *Spectator* remarked of *Adam in Moonshine*, which ran into
three impressions in its first year, that "the story is as credible
as a fairy-tale". And I thought, as I put aside the book and
stared out at the incredible ranges of factory and grimy hillside
streets from the diesel train that links Leeds and Bradford, that
no fairy-tale could possibly have taken root in these sooty
districts, over which a late November afternoon was hanging
its smoke-thickened shroud of silence. But I had forgotten the
moors that sweep away almost from the doorsteps of these
huddled industrial towns of the north, and it was from the
moors in all their weathers that *Adam in Moonshine* came. To
raise your eyes from a blank urban street and glimpse the hills,
soft and untenanted, beyond the rooftops: that was a reassur-
ance, an emphasis on magic, that the boy Priestley has never
forgotten.

   Much can be made of Priestley's obsession with magic; for
him the very word is among the most magical in the language,
and if you graze through his books at random it will not be
long before the four-leaved clover of magic leaps out of the page.

Generally rare in literature, this simple magic is common in Priestley, and although he may be thought to overwork the word, his moments of genuine magic, when the reader holds his breath and is compelled for a brief heart-touching moment to stop reading, are among the prose-writer's closest approaches to the purity and sheerness of a poem. A moment arrives in *The Linden Tree*, a play Priestley wrote just after the second war, when into the middle of a trivial back-and-forth family argument come the aching breath-taking sounds of the final theme in Elgar's cello concerto, and the moment is sustained in a long speech about the quiet soft summers of the past which the composer so poignantly regretted in that movement. The theatre is hushed, and a minute later the play proceeds; but something unforgettable has happened, and in memory that moment of magic suffuses the whole face of the play.

There are some books which are shot to pieces as soon as you try to summarise their stories on paper; like poems, they disintegrate under the cold eye of précis. *Adam in Moonshine* is a novel in this class. A laborious trailer, dotted with names of characters one forgets at once, could actually succeed in destroying the individual atmosphere or particular quality of the book, which might more readily be suggested in two calculated sentences of sympathetic criticism. It is hard to tell from a summary whether one would want to read the book, even harder to discover why one should read it. One of the most satisfactory critics of today, V. S. Pritchett, is stimulating because he has remained sufficiently amateur to let a book take control of his mind, to let it filter naturally into whichever channels of his personality it suits, and he can thereafter show what aspects of himself are served or pleasured by what aspects of the book. This is a deeply personal criticism which, conducted with respect and expressed with subtlety and grace, draws out the heart of literature. Such a method would be ideal for *Adam in Moonshine*.

The scenes dash away like fast cars in pursuit of each other; the thin silent Inspector, the melodramatic Baron, the shining gold-dusted girls, the chases by moonlight and the intrigues in

summer gardens, the false whiskers and the breathless conceal-
ments, all make the ingredients of one "glorious rich pudding
of the commonplace and the preposterous". Laughter is the
voice of the book, and its complexion is as fresh and its hair as
windswept as anything either Priestley or any author of his
generation has written. By the time I reached Bradford, had
settled into my room at the Victoria Hotel and drunk a cup of
tea in the lounge, *Adam in Moonshine* was finished and again
I had been enchanted by it, wondering how I could possibly
have forgotten how exciting and absurd it was. When recom-
mending it to a friend, was it enough simply to say that? Yes,
I thought it was. A mad, foolish, melodramatic story sustained
by a boyish capacity for adventure in a very young man who
flirts with three ravishing creatures all too beautiful to live, in a
countryside exquisitely evoked in the rampage of storm and
the wide serenity of sunlight: that was all I could say. A wrong
word or a slightly ironical tilt to an expression, and I could
squeeze the breath out of the book. That would never do. If
people came to stay with me, it would be safer to nod and
murmur a few words at the mention of the book, and later
quietly place a copy on their bedside table.

ON TIPTOE IN BRUDDERSFORD

One of my reasons for choosing to talk about J. B. Priestley
at Bradford was that for some time I had been angrily smoul-
dering at the treatment which he so frequently seemed to be
offered; hardly a reference occurred in the press which was not
either distantly respectful or misleadingly unkind. I had
noticed that many remarks which were passed about his work
could not be considered positively untrue, but were often
slanted in such a way that enormously derogatory implications
were suggested. If challenged, they faded cunningly from sight.
Absurdly prepared to imagine that the world of books was in
conspiracy against Priestley, I looked forward in accepting
Bradford's invitation to pulling aside the veil that concealed
such evil fallacies. The weather was right: a gloomy turbulent

day of wind and rain. In Yorkshire the Brontës were walking abroad, and I felt at home.

One's first visit to a place entrusted with the youth of an author one likes can be a rather nervous occasion, not unlike a return to one's place of birth after an absence of years. A mood of sentimental recognition had settled on me quite shamelessly as I walked across the cobbles from the acrid gloom of the station to the vaulted and solidly comfortable chambers of the hotel close at hand. I was conscious of a special longing not to be disappointed by Bradford, to be convinced that the picture was precisely as the novelist painted it. A form of high tea must be served; the lounge of the hotel would be populated by plump bespectacled businessmen obsessed by the price of wool. I settled back a shade smugly into my private thoughts, vaguely smiling as though I had just introduced someone to a fabled friend with whom I had spent the happiest days of my youth. The excitement was intense: this was a new world, yet I had been familiar for years with its reality and particular quality. I felt that high moment of superiority, which I believe comes to everyone who reads, when I was absolutely certain that nobody else in the world could possibly appreciate this rare incomparable flavour of living that I now shared with a writer. It occurs when an author's intention and a reader's understanding are faultlessly in tune; it occurred to me now, in the first smoky breath of Bradford.

Towards the hour of the lecture I drank some whisky to improve my confidence and was then agreeably met and welcomed by some officers of the society. As we drove to the technical college and I faced an audience much interested in books, it quickly became apparent that I had made a mistake. These people had read Priestley extensively, they knew the books well, probably even better than I knew them myself. Generally there are two occasions in the life of a book when its impact is true: at the moment of publication when the climate of the time makes its purpose clear and its inspiration sympathetic, and when the author has been dead sufficiently long to allow all impertinent considerations to depart from an

accepted estimate of his worth. The people to whom I was
talking had for the most part taken Priestley at the moment of
first impact; judgments could be spontaneous, unaffected, and
the atmosphere of criticism had not had time to be staled by
second thoughts much less reliable than first enthusiasm. I
doubt if I overrate the importance of enthusiasm in one's
reception of books, but there is often trouble in the aftermath.
Several writers recently, Kingsley Amis and Colin Wilson
among them, have been rocketed astonishingly high by critical
favour, only to be subjected within a few months to niggling
unfriendly attacks sponsored sometimes by jealousy but more
often by a desire—not necessarily misplaced but employing
the wrong weapons—to right the balance. It will be years
before the situation can be corrected, before an attempt can
be made on the truth: we are all too much involved in the
present.

Thus, to my ridiculous surprise, these people at Bradford
were still enthusiastic. They could recall, as I could not, the
precise effect which Priestley made with all his earlier books.
I had written a somewhat defensive paper, as though proposing
to address a quizzical sharp-featured dinner of literary critics at
a London club rather than a group of people devoted to the
reading of books without being called upon to write about them.
And I soon felt they did not really understand my attitude.
Perhaps, they might have said, Priestley is at the moment less
popular than he was at one time, but the reasons for that are
quite simple. *Festival at Farbridge* is not such a good book, after
all, as *Angel Pavement*, but the bulk of the books and plays have
not therefore decreased in value.

I saw my mistake and I regretted it. A writer's reputation
during his life is a pastime of the literary scene, an exercise for
critics, a pitched battle that moves further and further away
from its object; and the literary scene publicly thrives only in
the columns of a few newspapers, privately drawing its breath
and polishing its armour in a handful of Kensington drawing-
rooms, Soho restaurants and cocktail parties. A part of it
myself I suppose, I do not complain. I am only suggesting that

its apparent influence is something more than its actual strength. Writers do not mix satisfactorily together, for where each individual is a world in himself with laws and values and attitudes all his own, there can be no hope of such individuals cohering into a powerful and worthy society, each member feeding on the others. Horizons narrow, and gossip becomes the only possible intercourse.

I learned this at Bradford where they missed many of my references and could not even perceive the existence of that Parnassus, a mountain made out of a molehill, from which I took my attitude. I discovered that a docile audience, attentive but perplexed, had dislocated my approach and reset it at the correct angle. No anæsthetic was required; they treated me painlessly. But I felt faintly chastised for daring to speak loftily about Priestley in Bradford of all places, among the sort of people who had not only read his books but possessed the spirit which had made many of them what they were.

THE INVIOLABLE MOORS

Bright Day is the book where Bruddersford, always Priestley's strongest surge of inspiration, reaches that final perfection of handling, that climax, which always happens when a writer uses the same basic stuff of his experience, in one way or another, over and over again. He is unlikely to return to it now; it is off his chest. And Bruddersford, or Bradford, was the place I explored the following morning, when my ease of mind after the lecture seemed to be reflected in the pale relaxed sunlight that made the squares wider and the pompous municipal buildings more black with grime.

It was a black city, as though celebrating some devilish festival of commerce, a place that all seemed a part of its railway stations, smoky, faded, provincial, but in the grip of an atmosphere that was at once outmoded and cosmopolitan, like an urbane and rather heroic old gentleman who has retired from a business concern that covered the world. I felt that the town had lost much of its bustle, energy and significance; it seemed now no longer to be proudly self-contained, as cities and countries once were, but to be staring out towards its own suburbs as though the true life lay waiting there. One notices the same in London: if it is an ugly metropolitan civilisation we have made, we certainly take every opportunity to avoid being involved in it. We hurry to the suburbs, take trains to the country, creep into quiet homes. A civilisation on the run is almost worse than one which has fallen into decay.

Priestley, of course, was not to be found here, except in faint echoes that were more a product of the questing mind than of the town itself. On one of the hills that rise steeply from the centre of the town they were demolishing a fine chapel where once a wealthy piety had packed out the pews every Sunday; nowadays, it seemed, nobody came. The covered market resounded with the stray clatter of idleness, as though it were on the point of closing for ever. The trouble was, I felt, that Bradford paradoxically showed too little difference from its old self of forty years ago to be evocative of the moods and influences of atmosphere in which Priestley grew up. The imagination must be given a gulf to bridge before it can take wing, but here the facts had never seriously changed, though their focus and emphasis may have shifted a little. I found more of Dickens in an afternoon visit to Rochester: a century has passed and a different town stands on the foundations of the old. It is easier for distant atmospheres, attracted by the imagination, to drift up from the past.

I also made a hurried and ignorant visit to the moors, or at least to what I supposed were those tranquil areas of country into which many of the novels and essays are often serenely floating. I took a bus to Ilkley and tramped up a hillside rugged with wind; and it began to drizzle. Somewhat disheartened, I sat down under a tree with *The Good Companions* on my lap. I should, of course, have made the journey to Haworth. As soon as a dead writer becomes established in tradition he springs alive once more, and in succeeding generations the approach to him is clear and easy. A snuff-box or a scrap of handwriting can bring the Brontës to the imaginative surface of the mind much more surely that the whole of present-day Bradford can represent Priestley to the imagination, or Brighton suggest the atmosphere of *Brighton Rock*. These creations are too close to us; the two facts clash.

As a result of this visit to Bradford I felt once more the difficulty of undertaking a judicial study of the works of a living writer, and I was again aware of the danger of dissipating the strength of an opinion over several points of view; if one sees too many sides to every question, the mental fibres are allowed to fray and weaken. Even if a writer falls into temporary obscurity after his death, it is still possible for the critic to assume the state of mind in which total assessments and final judgments are made. But this cannot be done when the author is still so much alive that books and plays continue to pour from his study. Apart from the fact that an unexpected new work may surprise the whole of his previous output into a slightly different perspective, the man who writes about him, swayed a little by fashion and touched by devils of prejudice, may quite easily miss the rare oases of criticism as he wanders thirstily through the deserts of reviewing. While I had been going to bed that night in my Bradford hotel, I recall thinking that if ever I expanded my lecture into something publishable it must still remain informal, as though its pages were deep armchairs from which the argument gently proceeded.

SWITCH OFF THE DAY'S LONG CHAOS

On any bedside table, as well as *Adam in Moonshine*, I would also place *Benighted*, Priestley's second novel and published in 1927, for I like the intensity of the small hours and favour books which keep me awake in them. That night, after the lecture, with rain gusting occasionally at the window, I had read quickly through that short novel in shivers of scared comfortable loneliness. As the title suggests, the book belongs to the night, and its effect, its impact on the mind, takes flight as soon as the sun rises and the dark terrible winds are reduced to the milder breezes of dawn. The action is owlish, fixing you from the first page with its round hypnotic eye and releasing you, limp and exhausted by the tensions of melodrama, only when owls return to their barns and bats hang like shadows in the rafters.

People who have no taste for Dickens are often found to like *A Tale of Two Cities*, and in the same way *Benighted* seems to stand untypically apart from the rest of Priestley's fiction. Again it is only at the end, when a breathing-space gives one a chance to think about it, that one realises not only the shameless absurdity of all that has taken place—the ceaseless manufacturing of opportunities to frighten us out of our wits, the conjuring with all the screams and shadows, monsters and black storms, that ever occurred in those abandoned rectories of fiction built in the later years of the last century—but also the odd fact that Priestley has unobtrusively set against this somewhat flyblown backcloth the story of a tattered marriage that mends in the course of a single night. Not many words are used, just a few pointers, a glance here and there; but enough to make certain that this is the impression which remains, which stands clear of the book as soon as you put it down.

The nervy couple accompanied by their irritating friend, who find themselves marooned by floods on a Welsh hillside when night has already fallen, seem locked in the failure of their marriage. They have reached the state at which only separation can soothe their problems and bring them the hope of renewal. Yet Priestley, by shattering their nerves at every point with all the old devices, still surprising, of melodrama, succeeds in reducing their problems to nothing without sacrificing the conviction with which he has drawn his characters. Indeed, their reality as human beings, the simple fact that we believe in them, sympathise, feel warmly disposed, wish we could help them but cannot see a way out, makes the contrast which justifies as a different kind of reality the shrivelled madness of an old woman, the sinister lack of hospitality, the deathbed in a cobwebbed room of a man imprisoned in extreme age and dim memories, and the insane violence that screeches candle-lit down the rickety stairways. Once more it is the mixture of realism and romance: the latter makes the running, but the former survives well past the winning-post.

In the summer of 1936 Hugh Walpole said that "Priestley has a genius for the introduction of human beings who live absolutely from the first moment of our meeting with them". The characters in *Adam in Moonshine* are grotesques; they exist in the same half-way world as Bottom the Weaver playing Pyramus or transformed into the dunderhead lover of a fairy queen, a world where true flesh-and-blood creations gain a new dimension of reality from the glowing light of the magic or fabulous. By some further alchemy of the creative art, they become more themselves in becoming somebody else, they increase their realistic probability by entering an improbable sphere of fantasy. One feels that the people in *Adam in Moonshine*, when not involved in this particular adventure, are quite normal, and their normality is stressed rather than strained by the comic or fantastic masks they are expected for a spell to wear. They may be regarded in a way as bad actors concerned with immense verve and buoyancy in an amateur production, and I feel that this half-way world between pure nature and pure fancy—Bottom at one extreme, Pyramus at the other— is not only the place where extrovert writers come closest to the truth they seek and find the best material for its expression, but also happens to be well within the range of Priestley's particular vision of life.

For the theatre lies here: at one extreme, people and things and events, at the other, mummers, fancies, fairy-tales; in the middle, the theatre as we see it in *Twelfth Night* or *The Cherry Orchard*. Priestley is always exploring the half-light of that middle world where the sun is sinking away and the footlights dimly glow. Such an excursion he makes in a strange, moving tale (which also seems to have been written with special care), called *The Town Major of Miraucourt* in which the gross and frightful reality of the trenches in the first war is thrown back several centuries (indeed, out of time altogether) to join hands with the swilling, junketing circle of Falstaff and his friends.

The people, however, who dash out of the flooded night

F

into the apparent safety of a house in *Benighted* are neither grotesque nor caricatured; if anything in fact they are under-played, rather ordinary, so that although they "live absolutely from the first moment" we feel there is a chance we might grow quickly bored with them. A quiet-natured architect, his pallid wife and a rather jocose young man whose cracks rub Margaret the wrong way, are joined in their refuge by a wealthy businessman who speaks his mind (the kind of charac-ter Priestley himself is popularly imagined to be) and his bright young mistress. Against these people are ranged all the mad tricks and ludicrous terrors produced like a series of ghoulish parlour-games by the Femm family who occupy the house with Morgan, their dumb brutish servant. The interest of the book lies in the way these rather stock characters spring to individual life, develop and become persons, in conditions of such artificial extremity. The reader is aware that these circumstances are fabricated and rather a joke by the cold light of day, but he cannot talk away the sober down-to-earth reality of the five stranded people, and it is their fears and sudden reversals of feeling that echo in his mind, not his dim consciousness that Priestley has behaved rather naughtily in dragging out once more such faded and creaking props. It seems that the theatre has won; true drama has risen unscathed out of the hissing cauldron of the worst type of melodrama.

There is no writing in *Benighted*. The style is hasty, slapdash, and if for some reason I found myself briefly retiring from engagement with the story's unfolding and yet reading on, the prose seemed so loose-limbed that it was almost a displeasure to read it; one required something more precise. I occasionally feel a need to read prose for pleasure, without attending to its meaning, and for this, which offers a relief to the mind not unlike picking a tooth, it is essential to find a hard exactness of style which suggests that every word has fought for its place in the sentence. Such powers of mathematically stimulating the brain (and thereby oddly soothing it) lie in Hazlitt and in some of Henry James's less momentous hours. They are sometimes to be found in Priestley, but never in a book where the values he is trying to convey are human, not literary or intellectual. The style of his autobiographical chapters is a model of cleanliness in line and rhythm; the style of *Benighted* does not exist.

I put down the book, switched off the light and passed quickly into sleep. When I awoke, it was as though I had dreamed of meeting an ordinary but very agreeable young couple who would ask me to dine with them once every few months and whose marriage was now happy. I also felt, as I peered from the window into the gloomy canyon of the Bradford street below, much as Priestley must have felt when in 1927 he had briskly written two novels and had known that a challenge more commanding, monumental, lay in front of him. For this was the day I intended to spend, not only drifting about Bradford as I have described and perhaps out to the moors which winter would have swept bare of obvious colour, but also reading *The Good Companions*, which I had not read for some years and which had its heart, if anywhere, just here in Bruddersford.

THESE STUMBLING CHRONICLES

"If summat's done that you know isn't right, then start fightin' it like bloody 'ell bang off." This is a Priestley character talking; it is also Priestley. With a directness characteristic of the county of his birth, he never subtly implies his criticism of life, but designs his fiction to accommodate broad plain statements of a particular view. This view may often seem superficial because it is explicitly offered and picked out in its simplest terms; it is given depth, however, by the variety of invention and vigour of imagination that are placed at its service. A prime task of the writer is to simplify and make readily available a vision of life, but he is severely handicapped in producing this simplification by the fact that it is well-nigh impossible. His resources are complex and his art is beyond him: these are facts which every writer accepts with dismal resignation and only the excitement of conception enables him to ignore them. All serious writers launch into a new work with drunk minds, victims of the illusion that they can at last stuff all life between the covers of a single masterly book. Of course they fail; and I believe they live more disappointed lives than composers, who make a pattern of beauty that is absolute and need have reference to nothing but the spirit, and painters who are bound to a subject which the eye can encompass in a moment.

To be read at all the writer must simplify, compromise, and therefore admit failure in his heart of hearts every time he finishes a book. If your aim is partly that of a poet, to distil the essence of life, then like Virginia Woolf you avoid the direct statement and the conscientious narrative which will shatter your delicate laboratory. If, on the other hand, you are occupied with the somewhat coarser pursuit of discovering the nature of life, you will probably gain in power and certainly in readership if you make your statements as blunt as possible.

Arnold Bennett, who generally shows that he had a less complex reaction to life than Priestley and wrote books that rarely see beyond their overt and immediate subject, took his courage in both hands when he headed the last part of *The Old Wives' Tale* with the words "What Life Is". Although this was rather a reckless piece of showmanship providing a rod by which an irritable reader could measure Bennett's failure to live up to those three words, the impulse to fling back the curtains and speak quite openly was commendable and does not necessarily denote a total lack of subtlety and depth in the work of a writer who does so. Kafka, for example, never suggests great profundity of thought; his innovations are not philosophical, and his subtlety resides solely in the technique, in an originality of presentation which happens in itself to convey the spirit of his times. The disadvantage of this method, which is to be seen even more clearly in the work of Rex Warner, is that while we are given the opportunity to see a fresh vision from an unusual angle, even the most direct statement slips into ambiguity and is in danger of being weighed more heavily than it deserves. I enjoy these writers, but I am often inclined to overvalue them.

The Good Companions is a simple book, plainly constructed and straightforwardly told. Like so much of Priestley's work, its action begins on a note of rebellion, while its impulse is the search for romance without losing sight of reality; indeed, staring into the very heart of reality for the magic. Jess Oakroyd is pitched into loneliness by the drab quarrelling of his family, the scenes, the slapdash meals, the frayed tempers in rooms too poky to hold them. Miss Trant, suddenly relieved in early middle age of a burden that might have lasted her lifetime, turns against the trivial monotony of her genteel days in a Cotswold village. Inigo Jollifant, surrounded in the prepschool where he teaches by petty rulings, is refused permission to play the piano by the headmaster's wife, gets drunk and escapes into the night. These separate rebellions against the frustrations of life put the three characters convincingly on the road for what is probably the longest picaresque novel in English since *Pickwick*; judged out of the context of its time, it may also be thought one of the most satisfactory, for not just its chosen form but the nature of its material as well is episodic and therefore particularly well suited to picaresque treatment.

One of the faults of Dickens's early masterpiece—which is among the rare novels in which nothing can honestly be regarded as a fault—is the artificiality of the construction. One never quite escapes the feeling that Mr. Pickwick and his friends are being forced on their endless travels so that Dickens may introduce every comic incident and character that explodes into laughter in his mind. Priestley's material on the other hand, like that of *Don Quixote*, can only be handled picaresquely: the bulk of his characters are not wandering across England in search of amusement or to give their author a chance of displaying the breadth of his acquaintance with society, but to get a living and do their jobs. They are not amateurs of the road but professionals of the touring stage, and the fact that Priestley has decided to build a novel about their lives presupposes the use of a form which, though traditional in fiction, has often been regarded as more artificial than most, less like life. In the late twenties, in the context of its time, when fiction was almost exclusively looking for its shapes and patterns in a delineation of the inner life and not with narrative and outward plot, nothing seemed more hopelessly destined to failure than a long novel in a neglected tradition about the theatre. *The Good Companions* was, however, a phenomenal success, both popular and critical—too phenomenal a success perhaps—and this was in some measure due to the harmonious marriage of content and form at which Priestley skilfully officiated.

It was due in greater measure to Priestley's unique suitability to every aspect of the book's inspiration, development and scope. D. H. Lawrence's *Women in Love*, another gigantic conception of a very different level but the same decade, has to be admitted a failure on account of Lawrence's inadequacy to certain facets of his theme and certain spheres of his material: his efforts to depict the upper crust of society are ludicrous and severely wound our sense of the seriousness of the novelist's purpose; he knows Birkin more finely and at greater depth than he knows Gudrun, and the book is damaged by a final lack of contact between these two equally important characters; apart from the writing, which is always touch and go with Lawrence, the very vision is uneven. But although Priestley is infinitely far from attempting anything spiritually so ambitious as Lawrence, he is evenly in control of his work from the first moment and maintains the correct balances between all the ingredients he has chosen to mix.

A quick comparison of these two writers is bound to label one superficial and the other profound, on the basis of the aims each bears in mind when writing. But if it is a question of a work of art, which I hold *The Good Companions* to be, the profundity of a book lies not necessarily in the author's intention, but in the success with which he has unearthed the true and inevitable expression for that intention. Lawrence's thought in *Women in Love* is deeper than Priestley's ever could be, in the sense that Lawrence can move with passion and precise flashes of insight at levels to which Priestley's creative mind has no power of entry. But the confusion which dominated Lawrence, the violent and prejudiced eye which collected his material and presented it often with such ridiculous perversion, are defects which dominated the expression of his thought, sometimes came near wrecking it and gave it a superficiality which *in vacuo* it hardly possessed.

It would be critically absurd to compare the two novels I bring together here; they have nothing in common save that both are written in the same decade by two artists who differ extremely. But the portraits of life they draw are each equally true to one type of temperament, Lawrence's passionate and intellectual, Priestley's vital and optimistic. Some people prefer Lawrence, others Priestley; while some, according to their mood, feel there is much to be said for both. It is the marked difference of the two books I have mentioned that Priestley is more true to his temperament and purpose because he finds happier words to express them and a neater design to contain them.

There is no absolute truth to the secret of life, no key that anyone can turn in the lock. We glimpse behind the physical world suggestions of whatever sort the cast of our minds and the constitution of our emotions fit us to discover, and that is why one cannot discount a writer who, though one may read him with ease, never brings a quiver to one's nerves of recognition. Though Priestley has written books, particularly in the thirties, which strike the reader's mind with a false gaiety because he has calculated to entertain and appeared to present his entertainments with an air of lofty and avuncular patronage, he cannot be accused in his best works of falsifying what he sees with a view to making people jolly. When faced with Priestley's optimism, his humour and a riot of characters all making the most of their time, there is a temptation to say that life is not like that, when the truth is that one's own life happens not to be particularly like that; but life is like it, and like a good many other things too. One does not deny a writer his validity because his thought is sifted through a temperament and his vision coloured by a permanent attitude of mind. Occasionally Priestley is guilty of making the world seem supernaturally bright, like a music-hall in the blaze of finale, to keep the gallery on a roar. But his early novels, all his serious plays and one or two of the later books, share with *The Good Companions* that steady illumination of all sides, the bitter no less than the sweet, of the reality which Priestley clearly and individually sees.

It took me longer than I had imagined to read *The Good Companions* again and whenever I paused—first huddled under a pine-tree in a drizzle that swept in a curtain of gauze across Ilkley Moor and later when I caught the train back to London and spent several hours with it—I realised what a sad touching book it really was. The last sentence is fingered by a melancholy which has laid its hand over the entire action: "In this place," Priestley wrote, "whether we call it Bruddersford or Pittford Falls, perfection is not to be found, neither in men nor in the lot they are offered, to say nothing of the tales we tell of them, these hints and guesses, words in the air and gesticulating shadows, these stumbling chronicles of a dream of life." Once again, and it is not just here but lurking somewhere behind every page of the book, the presence of that autumnal melancholy can be felt, that faint subtle mist that goes straight to the heart, a vague sense of the uncertainty of life through which people move in loneliness like ghosts.

From time to time, when these people come together and the rafters ring, that disturbing presence is defeated and we experience the returning rush of confidence that is brought by rousing humour and the raising of glasses, but Priestley never lets the sadness depart for long. In fact it is on those occasions when he sends it packing and comes genially forward to show what a wonderful untroubled party his characters are enjoying that the feeling of slight unreality breaks in. It happens, for example, when the Good Companions first come together in Rawsley and excitably hold a dinner to celebrate their good fortune, and Priestley, moving suddenly forward into the present tense, seems to be pushing his slightly embarrassed characters into the centre of the stage to perform their comic turns and make us all glow with pleasure. We do not like to be hustled into humour as though it were a dose of tonic, especially when it contains a dash of sentimentality that suggests Priestley has momentarily retired from his characters and is therefore feeling a little self-conscious about them.

There are times like this when he appears to be relying too heavily on his facile powers of invention, to have devastated the surface of the scene with funny lines, and it is not surprising in so long and energetic a book that his imagination, where the finest comedy matures and the people really spring alive, should have occasionally loosened its grip and let him down. Most of the time he is involved up to the eyebrows in this "dream of life", but we trip over moments here and there—and they should be emphasised for many people are inclined to judge the book by them—when Priestley is no longer there among them, dreaming himself and being rattled this way and that by the same emotions, but has suddenly pulled himself together, realised that he is engaged in the lofty pursuit of writing a book and has at his command (he will treat them gently) a band of brave little people fighting the battle, smiling in the face of adversity and having a whale of a time. One or two such scenes drip the poison of embarrassment; they are fortunately rare.

A DREAM OF LIFE

The Good Companions consists of six hundred and forty pages. The first third, divided into six chapters, describes in detail the circumstances which caused three people, Jess Oakroyd, Elizabeth Trant and Inigo Jollifant, to take exception to their settled habit-hardened lives and dash off into the blue. From Bruddersford in the north, where the patient and philosophical Oakroyd is bullied at last into flying off the handle, from Hitherton in the west, where Miss Trant buys a car with girlish excitement and decides it is time for a holiday, from Washbury in the east, where even Inigo's buoyancy is punctured by the drab routines of prep-school life, the lines of these three adventures are closely traced until they meet at a point in the midlands, Rawsley, one early afternoon in October. And here they come across the dispirited remains of a touring

concert party who are sitting hopelessly in some refreshment
rooms, wondering what on earth to do next. Miss Trant
decides, unwisely, her heart bounding, that she will use her
inherited money to finance the company and put them on the
road again; Inigo, who is always sketching racy little tunes on
the piano, agrees that he will play for them; and Mr. Oakroyd,
a carpenter by trade, is asked if he will do odd jobs, build
scenery, work the curtain. For an exquisite moment they are all
happy.

But the high spirits of the second third of the book, when they
are all working together to make a success of the Good Companions in inconsequent market-towns, pretty resorts at the
end of the season, dark industrial places equipped with dusty
theatres and fourth-rate lodgings, are tempered not only by
the reader's growing realisation that he has been put among
rounded and fully articulated people who cannot be taken
lightly, but also by the fact that none of these characters has
yet achieved his ambition but is only marking time. This is
merely a stop-gap, quite amusing no doubt and very strange
but not gushing with the final happiness. Perfection, after all,
is not to be found. Inigo, careless of that gift to coax irresistible
tunes out of the piano, longs only to be allowed the chance to
write deathless prose. Lily, Mr. Oakroyd's daughter, is living
in Canada and he wants nothing more than to join her there.
Miss Trant is always conscious that this mad escapade is no
more than a holiday, just "a bit of life" as Miss Thong tells her.
Elsie Longstaff, the silly pretty soubrette, constantly keeps her
eye open for a "gentleman friend" who will pull her out of this
dreary round of bad meals, bored audiences and long Sundays
in the train. Then there is the pert and mocking face of
Susie Dean which cries out to be applauded in Shaftesbury
Avenue and the handsome figure, selfish and remote, of Jerry
Jerningham who is loftily aware that he is wasting his divine
talents on a godless traipse round the provinces. Only the old
hands, like Jimmy Nunn whose tired wisecracks proceed from
a wrecked digestion, and the much-travelled Morton Mitcham
who strums his banjo and reminisces about personal triumphs

on the far side of the world, only they rest content, for they have nothing left in their spirits to make the future bright.

Thus the third section of the book shows the gradual folding of this pack of cards, the relaxing of those impulses that brought them all together in the first place, so that tempers start fraying, uneasiness spoils their hours alone and the show begins to disintegrate. We are assured in an epilogue that most of them struggle another few rungs up the ladder of their desires, but such a conclusion seems to be provided in deference not to the mood of the book or the nature of life, but to the conventions of story-telling. If they have all gained something, however, they have lost something as well, and as one reaches the last page the prevailing sadness of the book offers its last gentle smile. To treat *The Good Companions* as a gross back-slapping novel of adventure and buxom humour represents a failure to glimpse the mood behind the frolic, the human loneliness that hovers over the bustle of event.

One of the reasons for this failure lies in the ebullience of the humour, the exuberance of phrase, the sharp, vital but not eccentric way in which the characters are fashioned. It is a tendency of Priestley's method to take the reader by storm and to rush him in a gale of laughter over the surface of the story; no one could be blamed for taking *The Good Companions* as a polished piece of optimism, designed to cheer the sinking heart and offer an escape from drabness and boredom. We envy those who can get drunk and rush out into the night, buy cars and drive away in them, jump on a lorry with an unknown destination, and we enjoy the release of reading about them. But this is the appeal of *The Good Companions*, not its power.

Humour is not a quality that grips; it relaxes. Our attention quietly settles into the backchat of a pair of comics or the riot of situations that twist in and out of a comedy film; and for that reason humour seems nowadays to have lost its gift of snapping the audience or reader into total attention, into that tense unbreakable condition of hypnosis which a tragic or a beautiful work of art can command. In the presence of humour one expects to be entertained, to make no effort, but to have laughter thrust into the mind as though we had a right to it; people always complain rather petulantly when they have failed to be amused by a particular comedian and they feel much more cheated than if they had remained stonily unmoved through a heart-rending tragedy of love. While watching a Chaplin film it is often hard to attach one's thoughts to the serious messages the piece is trying to convey beyond its laughter, and to do so one must reach closer to the piece, sharpen and direct one's attention. We cannot for some reason take humour seriously, as if it bore no relation to life.

Much of the humour in *The Good Companions* is external, incidental, a joke shared between Priestley and the reader, and although these asides and comic exaggerations lie respectably in the tradition of the humorous picaresque, they are often disconcerting, catching a character at a moment when he does not require that particular touch to make him live or occurring in such a way that we have to be dragged out of our absorption with the action to smile at the author's comment. From the very first, and quite rightly in such a tale, Priestley occupies the time-honoured position of a god presiding over the destinies of his people; in the opening sentences we are brought out of the sky above the Pennines and slowly glide down through the blue until Bruddersford appears in focus beneath our eyes. But as soon as this atmosphere of a brand-new world being opened to our gaze had been established by this method, the consistency of tone in the book would have been improved if Priestley had silently withdrawn to his dark tower and left the characters to make their own humour, to let the bubbles rush up from the depths to the surface and break naturally there. We are looking for defects and finding them; but they are small and scattered, pocking the book's face here and there but never eating away at its centre, and it is useful to remove them before moving on to discuss the virtues of this book which, if not Priestley's best, certainly forms the centre-piece of his reputation.

Priestley conducts his explorations mainly in the realms of behaviour, in outward appearances, in the things people do, the way they look, what they say, and the reader is left to divine, in the case of each character, the individual temper, the person within, that dictates these words and actions. If the character in question is truly drawn, albeit from the outside, the reader will become subtly aware of all that is happening in his mind and heart at a given instant. Cardboard characters, also drawn from the outside, possess no mind and heart and exist as people solely by virtue of the writer's vitality; even cardboard can relax its stiffness and move when touched by a phrase, but it will do nothing more communicative than move to order.

Of these two types of character, both products of the same methods, there is a mixture in *The Good Companions*. They are both equally lively, but only one of them lives. All the minor eccentrics, puppets shaped out of cardboard, respond to strings that are shivering with laughter, they dance as they are told, utter characteristic speeches, they are very entertaining, very vivid, but we never know them in the same way as the others. For we are not supposed to know them. Inigo's headmaster, constantly making a noise that Priestley represents as "chum-ha", the one-eyed pavilion-attendant at Sandybay, the purple and swollen Mr. Mord, Inigo's landlord at Tewborough, such figures are presented as though we were bumping full-tilt into them and had hardly a chance to see their faces; they make a brief impression, and vanish. And this is the effect they have on the other type of character—Inigo, Mr. Oakroyd, Susie, Miss Trant—whose adventures have put them into such an excitable state of mind that their reaction to the procession of eccentrics they encounter must have been very much like ours. They accept them in astonishment, but most of the time are too breathlessly busy to linger.

These are the people, slowly and patiently developed into fully realised characters, who create by their natures the situations which conceive the true rich humour of the book in their depths and throw it up so spontaneously that truth to life is consistently maintained. The chapter in which Mr. Oakroyd discovers that he is wanted by the police and for a spell thereafter is haunted by his innocent feeling of guilt wherever he looks is a superb example of this natural humour; once the situation had been conceived, it required no titivation, no comic make-up, none of the false whiskers of exaggeration. Priestley had only to report, quite straightforwardly, what happened; Mr. Oakroyd, whose character had been previously established, was suddenly put at the mercy of his nature and, by reacting characteristically, he not only added to his own weight and fullness in the reader's mind, but also quite incidentally produced the most exquisite humour. Again, an irresistibly natural comic scene occurs at a most improbable moment, when Inigo after listening enchanted to Susie on top of a clanking tram and then being told that she cannot return his love, bursts into pointless but uncontrollable laughter when Lady Partlit approaches them at tea in the hotel lounge. In one moment of explosive comic genius we are drawn deep within all three of them, and life is present in every detail of the scene.

Novels owe their existence to the human desire to tell stories and to listen to them, at one level or another, and ever since the eighteenth century, when Sterne sat remotely in his rectory caring nothing for the conventions he was expected to obey, a conflict has existed between what the readers might be supposed to want and what the authors positively wanted to write. Writers rarely launch into a book exlusively for their own delight and they never take their eyes entirely off the people who are going to read it. How differently Dickens would have written if he had not been committed by fashion to monthly parts; and even Meredith made some concessions to his age which crabbed the love affairs he described and went contrary to the morality he wished to imply. It is fair to say that writers are generally more interested in character and situation for their intrinsic appeal than in the simple progress of a story supported by characters and developed by situations, and that with readers the reverse is true. "I like a good story," they say; but most writers do not particularly care for a good story and as often as not cannot think where to find one.

That search tends to be the least rewarding, most coldly intellectual part of their job. Their equipment may be perfectly attuned to deal with every other aspect of writing, but for an ideal story they must wait and hope to discover it by chance, as Stevenson suddenly imagined in an instant the whole of *Dr. Jekyll and Mr. Hyde*. A writer is rarely expressed by his story; he must be content to express himself within it, without too much compromise but without pulling it too much out of shape. *The Good Companions*, an excellent story, was Priestley's chance to strike the balance between his own needs and wishes as a writer and the requirements of public taste. He was excited by the story itself and wanted to tell it without wandering from the point, as the execution plainly shows; that the public wanted to read it is proved by the sales figure and the household word. No one in England above thirty is likely to be ignorant of a book called *The Good Companions*.

We have spoken before of another balance that exists, between the nature of Priestley's talent and the type of material he has chosen to treat. As a result of this, he felt that the story could confidently be given its full head without any fear that it would go off the rails or totter to a standstill; the book is that much closer to life because it gives one no feeling of being confined within a given plot, no sense that any interesting matters have been withheld or that one has been given any unnecessary information. The generosity of design brings the reader a deep satisfaction as though the world had been turned inside out for him and he knew its secrets. About every encounter along the road, however brief—Mr. Poppleby and his dining-rooms, the buttonholding sentimental drunk in the train to Middleford—there is a certain inevitability, and we rarely get the impression that Priestley is squeezing a crank into every little gap in the narrative. Each of these encounters opens a fresh vista; down the corridor of each personality, sketched as sharply as lightning, we get a glimpse of it ranging behind the character, a world as exciting as the one we are already in and also vaguely belonging to it, a world about which five other novels no less vivid could be written. Such glimpses

enrich the action and then disappear, but not before they have
made their contribution to the cumulative effect of the book;
as a panoramic survey of England at the time, conducted
indirectly and mainly by implication, *The Good Companions* was
never bettered.

But these hurrying montages of people and events not only
broaden and deepen the book as a social picture beyond its
specified limits. Supported by its humour, they also enclose the
action within a cosiness and warmth of heart which, although
the spirit of the book is far from suggesting that we live in a
blissfully happy world, at least make a solid dependable place
from which we may listen in comfort to the rather melancholy
truths that are whispered to us. These, of course, may be
ignored, and the book may be approached in the mood of one
who releases the balloon from its moorings and rockets up into
the somewhat unreal empyrean of escape, where the warm sun
of humour hearteningly shines. But that, however pleasant,
is an injustice to the book, which owed its success in some
measure to two facts. It not only cheered people who were
recovering from a devastating war and an uncertain mingling
of gaiety and despair, with a robust and hopeful tale. It also, in
its background of sadness, anxiety, loneliness but a final philosophic calm, captured the mood of the time and tried to inter-
pret it.

When applied to a writer, humanity is a word so loosely
squandered by reviewers that it requires, if not to be redefined,
certainly to be emphasised before it is put to use. As more and
more novels are published every year, a host of such words
rattle out their anæmic praise in the newspapers and perform
no service beyond giving the publishers something agreeable
to quote in their advertisements. One cannot, however, write
about Priestley without calling the word into action; he is
humanitarian, humane and a humanist, and he writes with
humanity. Although his manner is frequently gruff and uncompromising and he makes no secret of it when he dislikes
types and attitudes, he possesses the essential creative gift of
instinctively knowing and being able to follow the threads of

correspondence between the outward appearance and behaviour of an individual and the often strikingly different inner
life he leads. He is aware of what it is like to be somebody else
and he can make the same indulgent allowances for him as that
person will silently make for himself. Such a gift of insight—and
the imagination of every constructive writer is both sharpened
and softened by it—breeds tenderness and sympathy, and
though without these qualities it is possible to write about people
with a snappy objectivity which brings to life, not them, but the
impression they have made on the writer's mind, like Voltaire
or Peacock or Aldous Huxley, no writer can create character
in emotional terms without their aid.

Just as one is often inclined to feel sentimental about oneself,
so a writer who is profoundly involved in his people often draws
close to losing emotional control about them, forgetting his
duty to convert the reader to a state of mind which will regard
those people in the same light. For the sake of proportion, tenderness and humanity must therefore be combined with an
almost cynical sense of the smallness of the individual's place
in the entire pattern of society and the world; and only then,
paradoxically, will the wonder and greatness of the individual
heart and mind be able to emerge without sentimentality, only
then will the reader be genuinely, irresistibly, moved. Novels
which minutely explore the individual on a closed circuit by
means of interior monologue and fail to relate him intimately
to the society in which he lives may be sensitive, instructive
and even tragic in their climate of feeling, but they are never
simply moving in the same way. Priestley has this pure humanity, this accurate sense of the world where men live together,
and a sympathetic awareness of many varieties of men who
live in that world. *The Good Companions* was his first novel
to display it.

Early in March 1927 Priestley was beginning to consider this
book. He had finished a dramatic version of *Nightmare Abbey*
which, though favourably entertained by Nigel Playfair and
J. B. Fagan, was never produced, and he had returned from
a holiday at Bandol-sur-Mer where he had been helping his

G

wife to write a Victorian domestic comedy. I mention these facts because they were Priestley's first attempts on the theatre and must have helped to wear down the rough edges of a technique that was already perfect when *Dangerous Corner* took the stage in 1932. But first there was *Benighted* to be written, and that occupied the spring; and then in July he was arranging to add *English Humour* to the English Heritage series J. C. Squire was editing. At the same time he was deciding to write the big novel next, and in the early autumn he was beginning to prepare for action. But he could not start writing it yet. In September he completed *The English Novel*, a brief and attractive survey which he had been commissioned to write in July, and after staying with Hugh Walpole in the Lake District, he had agreed to write a novel with his host, in the form of an exchange of letters; it was to be called *Farthing Hall* and they began work on it in October. On Walpole's part this was a characteristic gesture of kindness, for the sizeable advance of royalties which his name could command enabled Priestley during the following year to devote himself without financial anxiety to *The Good Companions*.

At the same time Priestley, anxious to begin wrestling with the giant that would occupy him for more than a year, was busy completing "the awful dreary grind" of *English Humour*, which was delivered in December, and by Christmas he was just writing his last *Saturday Review* essay for some time. There was nothing to finish in the New Year but about 10,000 words of *Farthing Hall*. Bringing this riot of activity at last to an end, he put everything aside and in January 1928 began to write *The Good Companions*, first at Church Hanborough, then during the summer at Deal in Kent and finally at 27 Well Walk, Hampstead, where the family moved in October. By May the first 100,000 words were complete; in July he had done 20,000 words of the second book, but it was not until the March of the following year that C. S. Evans of Heinemann received the manuscript in full.

The book, in which Evans strongly believed, was published in July, and in August when Priestley was on holiday at

Marhamchurch, near Bude, it was impossible yet to tell what kind of sale it would eventually have. The reviews came out in a blaze of eulogy; Ralph Straus, for example, found it possible to say in the *Sunday Times* that "here, indeed, is a truly great novel, which so far from being dead and forgotten within a season or two, will find more and more friends as the years pass by". Meanwhile Priestley, receiving numbers of letters from all kinds of people (an ex-missionary, Maurice Baring, the secretary of the BMA), doing no work at all in Devon, lolling on a sofa and smoking his pipe, was waiting to learn how far the public would go in support of the critics. By the end of August the sales had reached 7,500. The figures increased and within a month the book had roared past the point where a modest success would have stopped it. In October Priestley began work on *Angel Pavement*, and by the time it was published, in August of the following year, its predecessor was still selling between one and two thousand copies a week. In the weeks that led up to the previous Christmas, 5,000 copies a day were despatched from Heinemann's warehouses.

That is the story, in brief, of *The Good Companions*; it was equally successful in America and has been translated into most languages. It enjoyed considerable success on the stage when Priestley dramatised it with Edward Knoblock, and Julian Wylie put it on at His Majesty's in May 1931. Two films have been made of it; the book has been steadily bought for twenty-eight years. Usually absent from library shelves, still frequently asked for in the shops, handsomely entertained in the memory of the generation for whom Priestley wrote, popping up in anthologies of prose and providing schools with passages for translation into French, nowadays often mentioned to prove a point in argument by people who have never read it, rarely admitted to the index of studies of modern writing, *The Good Companions* established Priestley so firmly as a man purveying racy narratives salted by homespun humour in the traditional way that his reputation has never recovered from the shock. Every time he wrote another book, there was a tendency to feel disappointed that the mixture had changed, that Priestley had nipped smartly round another corner and was exploring forms, techniques and attitudes quite different from those that produced *The Good Companions*.

Nobody can be blamed, neither critic nor public nor Priestley: a success so overwhelming as *The Good Companions* inevitably becomes the measure by which all subsequent performances are judged, and the points it made about Priestley's talent registered so deeply in the public consciousness that he was always afterwards accepted as someone married to the attitude of mind, cast of vision and type of humour which those points implied. A piece of writing with an explicitly serious purpose was liable to be taken as a case of the clown playing Hamlet; a novel which showed a gleam of humour would be regarded as an attempt to cash in on the previous success. Yet all the time, illogically, the press would beseech Mr. Priestley to return to his former mode, to the spiritual home of the "comic-romantic epic". Even in 1946 Monica Dickens could write, "I mourn the lost magic of *The Good Companions*. Will Priestley ever recapture it?"

But except occasionally when he seemed rather lazily to accept the popular estimate of himself as a good-hearted comedian with escape routes to offer (in writing *Let the People Sing*, for example, just before the war), he has never wanted to recapture it, for his is essentially a ranging talent that demands new ground to break. It is understandable that versatility can seem more of a curse to a writer thus burdened with the weight of a particular success, branded by a gigantic reputation. An ideal career in letters rises steadily to a climax; irrespective of true values, it is human nature to ensure that what began with a bang will end with something of a whimper. I am not suggesting that *The Good Companions* was notably inferior to the work that followed it. I merely think it a pity, from the point of view of Priestley's serious reputation as a writer within his own time, that the book burst so early in his career. His critics invariably look back to it, some with honest regret, others with indolent misunderstanding.

"Mr. Priestley," wrote Kay Dick in the *Spectator* in 1955, "a jolly type with a pipe, is a man we can wholly understand." Jess Oakroyd, too, was a jolly type with a pipe, and Priestley can only be wholly understood at this level by those who never read his work.

A writer can rarely be said to make a reputation for himself. It is something pinned to his breast or scribbled on his back, frequently bearing little relation to his deserts, and to be sensibly regarded more as an occupational risk than a cool appraisal of his value. If he happens to be a public figure and utters a word out of place, the tide of popularity will turn against him. If he times a book so that it satisfies a momentary fashion, his work will be accorded a value beyond its strength. When it seems that a writer is established in a certain mode and has received due credit for his efforts therein, a reaction is bound to follow: generations follow one another more swiftly than individuals, times change more rapidly. The atmosphere of fashion is always youthful; the new is preferable to the true; what was believed ten years ago and considered of worth is unlikely to answer the needs and demands of today. There is something to be said for the philosophical notion that the past and the future are more mature than the present, which is an untried adolescent time. It is a time when writers whose claims to mature critical evaluation were established in the past and are now buried in it, sink into a drab respect or rise, in their continuing efforts to speak for their age, to face denunciation.

Priestley was at the height of his reputation far too early, in the middle of the thirties. Having granted its full approval, one cannot help feeling that criticism would have liked Priestley to retreat, to retire from literary activity as once E. M. Forster did. Some years after Galsworthy's death a critic spoke of "the novels he wrote endlessly until he died", and that impression of a dreary machine incessantly churning out its unwanted products is bound to follow after a writer has received extreme honours. To some extent this has happened to Priestley, and I only complain because the false judgment implied in this state of affairs has the effect of hiding his best work from many people who would find it a source of pleasure.

But when you open *The Good Companions* and begin reading and sail gently down out of the sky above the Pennine Range and find yourself in Bruddersford being jostled along the Manchester Road towards tea-time on a Saturday, these things hardly seem to matter very much. The tangles of opinion, the screams and whispers that issue from the thickets of the literary scene, are snapped into silence as soon as you pick up the book. Then, for some hours, you are alone as you read, and while you ignore the sounds of night and hear nothing of the clock, every chamber of your mind is invaded by a host of sure-footed characters, people you will later recall and imagine you once knew; your interest will be carried along at a sharp trot on the backs of young and vigorous images which chase across many counties. *The Good Companions* makes you forget, yet you emerge from it with your mind quickened to life, not feeling that you have been pleasantly deluded by a lily too brightly gilded.

But it is an impertinence in criticism to tell people what their reactions will be to a book, for they will deny it whatever the cost; I can only record my own. Much of this I have already done, but I remember when I finished the book as the train from Bradford was beginning its long clanking run through the northern suburbs that my mind became curiously filled with idle scraps of thought which echoed trivially there. The book was one year older than myself, I thought. What was that surging eloquent piece about jazz when Jerry Jerningham first tap-danced on to the stage in a dirty Midland hall? I wondered vaguely what time it was, whether my typewriter had been stolen. Was Priestley sitting in a garden when he wrote the last words and did he then pour himself a drink—whisky perhaps? I would have a whisky myself at King's Cross. It was as though the book had pushed everything I owned, the people I knew, these hours on a chilly Thursday night, out to the distant, almost subconscious limits of the mind, and after planting its deep roots in the centre, was determined to stay there. One should take a while to recover from a book; for that is the time, when the dream is still buzzing in the mind and looking for a place to settle for good, when the depth of its impression is determined and one's opinion solidly formed. By the time I was splashing ginger ale into the promised Scotch, I was hearing voices around me again and could glimpse myself rather unreally in a mirror behind the bar. I listened to the voices and slowly began to wonder who owned them. This, after all, was the world about which *The Good Companions* was written, even if it did all happen in the year before I was born.

V. A Best-Selling Author

A MAGIC CITY

I HAD first read *Angel Pavement* in the Royal Air Force, where I would sit at my desk with the middle drawer half-open and the book balancing on a litter of pencils, rubber stamps and routine orders, so that when someone came into the room, by an abrupt and heaving effort of the stomach muscles, I could close the drawer and look as though I were pondering some knotty problem of discipline or administration. Pinned down in Lancashire through a windy winter, I remember the book made me feel sick for London, and I was somewhat irritated by the failure of the characters to appreciate their freedom to roam the streets, attend concerts, make plans that would not be defeated by the sudden rearing of an idle regulation. But now, after coming back from Bradford and returning to work, I felt I should read the book again, partly because I recalled a relaxed and leisurely design which had been particularly to my taste amid the restrictions of the service, and partly to see how it faced up to *The Good Companions* while that book was still fresh in my mind. I bought a first edition at Foyle's—so bulky that it spoilt the shape of my brief-case—and began reading it on my journeys to and from the office, under the malevolent gaze of standing men on the District Line who felt they had a better title to the seat I occupied.

One first notices that the general technique bears a close resemblance to that of *The Good Companions*, except that Priestley, no longer the conjuror pulling out of the hat characters and events even stranger than white rabbits and occasionally accompanying the performance with some patter of his own, has withdrawn a little further and seems intent on building up an objective picture, detail by detail, of a city he had closely studied: London. Almost from the beginning, despite small touches of humour, it is evident that the novelist's purpose is more serious and his mood more sombre. He moves his readers into the atmosphere of London just as gently as Bruddersford opens to our gaze in *The Good Companions*, but the guiding hand is less personal and for some time we cannot be sure of the expression worn by the author's face.

A ship from a Baltic state is tying up one evening in the Pool of London, and aboard, hanging over the rail and staring ruminatively across to Cannon Street Station and the dome of St. Paul's, there is a balding figure with a giant moustache and a good but ill-fitting suit. Nobody catching him at that moment would quite be able to fathom him, decide where he belonged, what he was doing there. An adventure is in the air, a shade sinister, vaguely whispering its possibilities at the back of this Mr. Golspie's unaccountable mind, and as we follow this figure off the ship, watch him climb into a taxi and see the "tiny answering gleam in his eye" as the lights flash past his windows, we are made to feel that those possibilities are endless and will soon be touching a number of lives that are as yet drably unaware that a man with dark foreign thoughts and vodka on his breath has crept quietly into London by night.

This prologue is the aperitif; one is now hungry for the meal and although the ingredients are basically simple and would hardly be thought to have the strength to sustain such a lengthy feast, all the trimmings are present, the spices and the details, which Priestley much more sternly kept at bay in his previous novel. For the action is not designed in quite the same way: it is looser, more expansive. Certain major parts of the book are attached to the governing thread by the lightest associations. The individual strands that begin *The Good Companions* are all gathered together, joined to others and bound into a single thread, which prevents the narrative from falling into diffusion; it is so powerful that it makes every incidental occurrence appear relevant to it. But the central thread that pulls the various parts of *Angel Pavement* together is first of all the office where the characters somewhat reluctantly work, and secondly Mr. Golspie who elbows his way into all their lives and forcibly gives them an inter-relation rather tighter than the humdrum casual contacts of their normal routine. The disadvantage of this is that the novel never fully integrates one's interest, and small adjustments of attention are necessary all the time; when in the company of Turgis, for example, one wonders what is happening to Miss Matfield, and Miss Matfield's links with Turgis are so slender and cursory that we feel rather lost, unattached suddenly, as though she no longer belonged to this world. Regarding the book as a piece of construction, therefore, one senses this lack of a total tension which, in unifying the various elements in the design, also unifies and concentrates the interest of the reader. It looks as though Priestley had planned out a series of short stories, discovered one or two points where they could be made to join and eventually brought them all into the orbit of another short story: for Golspie's cheating practices, developing with a slow and tantalising ease through the length of the book, in one way or another affect all the characters, Turgis, Miss Matfield, Mr. Smeeth, Dersingham, even the office boy. But happily there is more than one advantage to this method, and they far outweigh any dissatisfaction one may feel with the slight awkwardness of the plan.

To begin with, Priestley is set at liberty to fulfil his true purpose in writing the book. The story is never for a moment his first concern. Zola's method, in preparing every novel in the Rougon-Macquart series, was to determine the particular class or district or profession of which he wanted to present a naturalistic picture, discover by close research every detail that went to its composition, and only then piece together a story that would enable him to show its every aspect in the clearest light. The narrative is simply there to keep the reader's attention focussed, while the book more subtly does its work on the mind. The same method might have been used for *Angel Pavement*, for the story resembles a jigsaw cut into such large and simple fragments that a child, given the pieces all at once, could complete it in a few moments. But Priestley hands out these pieces slowly, one by one, just sufficiently often to prevent us turning away, thus persuading us to examine the detailed picture of life which is the real content and purpose of each piece, before we fit it into the pattern. When finished, the whole puzzle is intended to present a panoramic view of middle-class London, and in that object the book succeeds.

ON LIFE AND LUCKY BAGS

Angel Pavement is an alleyway in the city where Twigg and Dersingham, who are engaged in supplying veneers to the furnishing trade, have their office; Mr. Dersingham, with his thinning hair, weak blue eyes and amiable manner, is in charge, and his staff consists of Mr. Smeeth, mild and frightened, good at figures and living in the suburbs, the sulky and pimpled Turgis who is a clerk and has lodgings in Camden Town, Miss Matfield, the brisk sensible secretary who feels very grown up; Mr. Goath, the mournful traveller; and Stanley, the office boy. This firm, in the bland but ineffectual control of Dersingham, is in danger of going out of business when Mr. Golspie suddenly appears on the scene. An atmosphere at once gathers round this exotic figure.

It seems that he will magically bring prosperity back to the firm; he holds a monopoly of certain cheap materials in foreign parts. Loud, heavy and vulgar, his influence tramps its way into the quiet but rather desperate lives he has interrupted. He attends a catastrophic dinner-party at the Dersinghams' flat off the Gloucester Road; he becomes a figure for speculation in Hampstead where Miss Matfield lodges in a dreary hostel for women, and he later launches into a somewhat avuncular affair with her, sweeping her round London at impressive expense; he patronises Mr. Smeeth whose hopes of preferment pathetically soar; while his ravishing daughter, Lena, entraps poor Turgis in a hopeless love. Then, with money in their pockets, Golspie and Lena disappear. Jobs are lost, hearts are broken, the future seems to be torn across with despair. But

Priestley has not yet finished; again he makes a concession to the happy ending and all these people, as though purged of their weaknesses by a dirty biting wind from across the North Sea, slowly find their feet and approach the problems of their lives with a much wiser and more confident step.

One requires only to make certain reasonable comparisons between the people pursuing their days in this dark wintry London and those who danced lightly from place to place in *The Good Companions* to appreciate the difference in tone and realise the change of attitude. Although this is a long novel like the other and contains its quirkish characters and decoration of humour, Priestley has already turned away from the faint and tolerable melancholy of the human condition which can be eased by gently breaking out of it from time to time, and he has entered a mood in which the temper of life is tragic, fateful and lonely. In a way, as we have seen, this is a less personal novel, for one can discern the workings of the comic temperament in a book more readily than a tragic attitude. In their purest forms, comedy is an expression of personal vision, tragedy of the cosmic: this may be illusory, for all art is deeply personal, but it is a distinction true to the impression which work in those two categories leaves in the mind.

It is also a distinction, however, which is not strictly to the point, because *Angel Pavement* does not discover its grandeur in the fact that its home lies in the higher reaches of tragedy. Priestley lacks the intensity to struggle there, and never tries. But to view the book from a standpoint roughly opposite that which gives the truest picture of *The Good Companions* enables one to see how much less personal it is in this sense, how much less warm and reassuring, more reserved and cautious in the approach to its implications. Another advantage of the loose-limbed action, in which the parts are only just close enough to remain conscious of each other, is the emphasis it places on the emptiness and terrible solitude of these people who move like ghosts through the racket of an urban civilisation, thirstily drinking at pools of fantasy, somehow keeping alive behind their grey worried faces, hoping against hope.

In another sense, too, the book is infinitely more personal than anything Priestley had attempted before. For he felt it more deeply; brought to its writing a much finer and more penetrating eye, an even deeper fund of tenderness and humanity, because he was concerned. Jess Oakroyd, burdened by a family and fatigued by his trivial round, was suddenly visited by the strength of mind to tear up his insurance card and walk away; Mr. Smeeth, also a quiet-natured and untalkative family man who smoked a pipe and respected the established order, could never find it either in his nature or his circumstances to take such violent action. Inigo Jollifant's temperament, casual and flushed with energy, enabled him without a tremor to take steps which Turgis would have found impossible; yet they are both young men with romantic ideals and a relish for the unexpected. Miss Trant, moneyed and free as air, was in a position to perform miracles of freedom for herself, but Miss Matfield, slightly younger but much the same type, never even considered the possibility of not looking for another job when Twigg and Dersingham let her down. This is another world, where the problems are more urgent and the people unhappier, more passive, less able to look after themselves. In Priestley they called forth a quality of gentle, almost chiding concern, these people dominated by a massive city whose operations they could not understand and where they could never find what they wanted, and they also seemed to harden in his mind a determination to conquer in words the menaces of which they were dimly conscious.

In *Angel Pavement*, through the eyes of his characters, Priestley is laying out the chilly hostile lengths of London streets, packing the buses and tubes with unmoving faces, filling the palatial tea-shops and vast cinemas with people seeking their paradise, opening doors on hundreds of metropolitan lives that are fatuously, emptily or falsely conducted. Irony controls his voice as a rule, but occasionally anger or sorrow splits it into a roar so loud that for a moment the character we are with is ousted from the scene. If Priestley were merely indulging a taste for fine surges of language or sweeping attacks on the institutions of his time, we might be able to forgive his violence but we should be unlikely to read on. As it is, the sensational descriptions are geared to the perceptions of the characters, which naturally turns London into a cruel embittering place as well as a city of dreams, splendid and remote from its own dispirited bustling.

Sir Ifor Evans has pointed out that Priestley belongs to the long tradition in English letters which has created literature out of its genuine detestation of poverty; but it was only indirectly as a social reformer that Priestley wrote *Angel Pavement*. The apprehensive years after the depression, the moods of fear, the hanging on to an existence hardly worth keeping, are captured in the book. They are not, however, turned into an opportunity for proposing changes and castigating the responsible. Priestley has not yet taken to preaching, for he is much more engaged in the difficulties of living, the inner tangles that an individual can only sort out for himself, than in the problems of society which require a political solution. *Angel Pavement* may be regarded as the imaginative companion-piece to *English Journey*, which is a factual survey of this country during the early thirties; the mood of the two books strikes the same chord, in a minor key, disturbingly. But the novel is about isolated people living in a city, and the problems which occupy their suffering hours will never be quietened by social reform. Mr. Smeeth is doomed to worry for ever about getting the sack and making ends meet; Turgis will drift into gloomy fantasies about girls; young women like Miss Matfield will always sourly wonder how on earth they can make something happen.

If the individual triumph of the book is Turgis, that lonely, stilted and unprepossessing young man, a prey to dashing fantasies, who is suddenly faced with a reality too wonderful to swallow, the grandeur lies not merely in the breadth and depth of which the design is capable, but in the particular way Priestley has exploited that design. He neither pricks out a close and ingenious pattern of details to compose, by cumulative effect, the entire picture; nor does he sweep impressionistically across the canvas. His gift rests somewhere between these extremes of method, so that he is capable of selecting the correct sort and the right number of details to make his descriptions appear plainly naturalistic and at the same time, to make the impact more violent on the reader, with the help of understatement, exaggeration and a calculated crescendo to the climax, he can leave the impression that he has merely daubed the canvas with a few deft splashes of paint. Zola vouchsafed too many details, and his work is saved only by the brilliant texture of the language; he tells us a good deal that we do not especially want to know. On the other hand Graham Greene, who relies on the one crucial detail that will snap a scene into perfect focus, often leaves us wishing that we knew a little more. In *Angel Pavement*, Priestley's descriptions not only satisfy curiosity by pouncing on details and exposing them but also rise to flights of language which pull the reader irresistibly into the thick of the atmosphere. His territory spreads all over London, from Maida Vale through the West End to dockland, from Earl's Court across to Camden Town and Hampstead, and the subtle mood of all these regions, their secret essences, are perfectly caught and knitted into the action. Such an obsession with places and weathers on a writer's part can often drive humanity away, but save for brief moments, the characters, though dominated by London in their lives, climb on top of it for the purposes of narrative, and Priestley never relaxes in his tender and patient study of them. They emerge from that metropolitan welter like shadows, are seen in their full truth for six hundred pages and then once again sink back into the dark. One remembers them.

It is a better book than *The Good Companions* because there is more of Priestley's heart in it, more of his serious concern, though perhaps less of his affection. Starting in October 1929, he wrote it throughout the winter in London and then at Kingswear in Devon, where he managed to produce at the rate of about twenty thousand words a week. The book was finished in April 1930 and published in the following August, when it received a welcome quite as warm as that accorded its predecessor. A few years later it became the representative volume of his work to be included in the Everyman's Library, and this suggestion that the book at least deserves a chance to be considered of classic status confirms my own belief that it is the most moving, actual and well-stocked of his novels. A possible rival exists in *Bright Day*.

THIS EARTH OF OURS

He asked very little for *Faraway*, the tale which followed *Angel Pavement* in 1932. After reading a few pages of it I remember putting it aside as a novel suitable for convalescence, to help pass the long white days of an illness in a flurry of adventure. For *Faraway* is a straightforward and conventional piece of yarn-spinning in the tradition of the adventure story and the basis of the plot is the simplest and least original of all Priestley's novels. William Dursley, a tolerably prosperous maltster in a dull Suffolk town, finds his routine upset by the visit of a brandy-soaked blustering uncle who appears one wet night with stories of the south seas, schooners, lagoons and the deep blue skies. For a while nothing happens; the uncle stays, William is faintly troubled with the feeling that something is about to happen like "a fuse burning quietly along the ground". Then a woman as exotic as a parakeet and a man as shady as a pirate appear on the scene, talk secretly with the uncle and, in William's absence, drunkenly roar through his house one night and then vanish. This orgy proves too much for the uncle who confides a deathbed secret to his nephew: three people who have done him good turns, including William, must share his discovery of an uncharted South Sea island which he called Faraway and where he discovered an enormous quantity of pitch-blende, the ore from which radium is drawn.

The other two, whom William goes out to find, are Commander Ivybridge, quiet, thin-lipped and retired, and a certain P. T. Riley who lives in San Francisco. Ivybridge sails south with a broad-faced Lancashire businessman called Ramsbottom, and William sails west and travels across America, only to find that P. T. Riley is the gay sophisticated daughter of the original Riley his uncle had known. Together they set out, William enchanted, to join their partners in Tahiti, and they move slowly through the islands in the search for Faraway. But they find it too late: their rivals, those bright sinister creatures who cropped up at the beginning, have reached it first. Suffering, disillusion, privation and loss, accumulate towards the end to kill the adventure and turn it into a nightmare. The Commander loses his life on Easter Island which he has always longed to visit; P. T. Riley slips through William's fingers into the oily hands of a film-star; Ramsbottom, that bluff insular character who appears very movingly in contrast with his exotic surroundings, has suffered so darkly from the enterprise that he is delighted to return to gentle routines of provincial commerce. As usual in Priestley's novels, the stormy seas in which tragedy almost overturned the vessel calm down in the end, and even a pale gleam of sunshine appears.

These lunges out of routine which are at the core of much of Priestley's work, his plays included, are a momentary human attempt to defeat fate, to taste the alien excitement of a life for which one is not permanently fitted. As far as the writer is concerned, they are not so much realistic in themselves as rich in opportunities for realism; apart from the fact that he can create his world from a wide selection of places and atmospheres, in *Faraway* as in *The Good Companions*, they add to the stature and veracity of characters by showing them acting out of character.

Priestley had sailed for his first visit to America in February 1931 and after spending some time in New York, giving interviews and not getting the right amount of sleep, he moved westwards on a lecture-tour and arrived at Hollywood in March. From San Francisco, which is beautifully described in *Faraway* as the place where William fell under the dazzling spell of P. T. Riley, he sailed south for Papeete, for much of the journey in the grip of a serious illness which a drug-taking doctor did little to improve: these cannot have been ideal conditions for collecting the sunny extravagant material that went into the extended sea-scapes and island pictures of *Faraway*. Priestley's

H

writing, rarely to be called stylish in the sense of an instrument graceful and decorated to serve the cause of pure beauty, is at its finest in these later chapters when the moods of the ocean are trapped and the strange varying loveliness of the islands is put up to hang in a gauze of words.

Once or twice in *Angel Pavement*, though never in *The Good Companions*, the writer of gentle atmospheric essays appeared to push the novelist aside for a moment and pause for reflection, and in *Faraway* this is happening quite often—so often in fact that it offends the reader who is thirsting for the tide of the story to begin flowing once more. Once again there is no denying that the tale could have been more briefly told. The beginning, as usual, proceeds to establish the characters of the book as casually as if we were meeting them in life (the method is sound for it builds up an enormous reserve of affection for them), and we have read almost a hundred and fifty pages before the excited adventurers find themselves aboard a ship. Up to that point the interest in the narrative has been incidental; if Priestley cared more about the expedition itself, he would have hurried the planning forward and given a desperate feeling of urgency to the enterprise, but he cares only for the characters who happen to be involved in it and the slow plodding scheme of existence in William's sleepy town, the retired life of naval officers rusting away in small coastal resorts, the state of mind in which a coarse and liverish north-country businessman generally finds himself, these concern him much more intensely than a dubious errand to the south seas for an island covered with pitch-blende. At the time his method of displaying character seems superficial, using quite ordinary dialogue, leaving things unsaid, describing a gesture or a passing thought, but the preliminaries over, when the character turns and begins to sail into the wind of the book and play his part in the action, one realises that he has unobtrusively become so complete a person (and above all a person set within a society) that one can reliably imagine how he would react in any given circumstances, though not always in such unexpected ones as Priestley often devises for him.

When the journey towards the tropics begins in *Faraway* the narrative continues to be incidental, but from another point of view; now it is not the characters but the landscapes, the weird towering islands, the unimaginable atmospheres rising out of the seas, which dictate the speed at which the story runs. The language itself lifts above the gentler tone that carries the narrative. But these descriptions are not merely used to create a background against which the action can be played, for in a curious and haunting way they echo the mood and fortunes of the little expedition and strangely infect their minds. J. C. Squire pointed out that tragic issues were not avoided in this novel, "nor wickedness, nor squalor, not the vulgarisation of the world, nor the incomprehensibility of evil", and by an odd association of the mind all these forces intruding on the serenity of that fabulous region—the film company in Tahiti, the sleazy night-clubs, the natives growing sly and sophisticated—become linked with a sense of the failure, the disappointment, the sadness of the expedition, even before we know how it will end. Priestley has accomplished in fact a perfect fusion of elements which keeps the novel in the modern world and away from the pure escapism we might have expected from a novel with such a plot.

It is a near thing, however, for so trivial a story was bound to tell against him, and the reviews of the book when it first appeared were very mixed. You could think, for example, that Priestley had neither the staying power nor the creative genius for long-distance fiction, that his characters were stock dolls from nineteenth-century literary nurseries, but you could also, just as outspokenly, hold the view that this was the fullest, richest and profoundest novel by an author who combined a special literary insight with a worldwide appeal. Twenty-five years ago, as now, reviewers were implicitly insisting on the principle that their words should be read more for entertainment than for guidance. To say with respect to this novel that Priestley "becomes a public danger when he proclaims, almost truculently, that all's well with the world" is to launch an absurdity which nothing that Priestley had written by 1932 can be made to support except on the most perfunctory reading. He is a writer nearly always denied his undertones; that gruff north-country voice is deceptive.

I had to wait quite a long time before I was ill enough to read *Faraway* and then I was recovering from mumps, not smoking, my vanity refusing visitors because my face had swollen to look ludicrously like Ramsbottom's, and pouring the days away between the covers of fat books. I found it ideal, for it contains a sense of the wide world and you can breathe deeply within its long slow development. Great draughts of Priestley are more just to his method and talents than the polite little sips which reading in buses or snatching a few pages before sinking into sleep can give you. He works in long sequences, which, if interrupted, lose some of their virtue.

HOWLING TO THE STARS

Wonder Hero, which followed *Faraway* in 1933, shows a marked decline in importance and might be regarded as a jaunty, extrovert sketch for the novel that succeeded it, *They Walk in the City*. Charlie Habble, an engineer in a Midland town during the bleak weather of the depression, is ballooned to briefly heroic proportions by a daily newspaper short of a story. This time the land of romance, as offered by contemporary society, is ironically portrayed: the luxury hotel, the insane helter-skelter of newspapers, the brittle and silly hysteria of cocktail parties and night-clubs, and the attempt of these heady delights to overwhelm a fresh clear-eyed lad from the Midlands gives Priestley an opportunity to show them as they inevitably appear to the outsider, empty, incomprehensible and somewhat degraded. Among the cynics, egocentrics and drunks, the only people Charlie meets who make him feel at ease are the odd chambermaids and footmen who serve him in his new-found glory; and also a young woman from his own district who has been chosen by another daily newspaper as the beauty queen. In the turmoil of his closely organised days, Charlie catches only an occasional glimpse of her, but this is enough to assure him that she is the most beautiful thing in the world.

Then suddenly, with terrible contrast, the scene changes, when Charlie receives an appeal from an uncle in Yorkshire to visit his ailing aunt, and disappearing without a word from the wealthy fatiguing tumult in London he takes a night train and arrives in a dead and unhappy town where the factories are idle, the men are grey and restless, the women and children half-starved. Priestley makes the switch very convincingly; the hollowness of romance has enabled Charlie, who before had taken the real world around him idly for granted, to see where that world was going, what its difficulties and dangers were and how he could act to improve them. After getting his aunt into a convalescent home and helping the family with the money given him by the newspaper, he returns to London, only to find that the world which had so extravagantly put its wealth and honour at his disposal for a few days is now closed to him for ever; the story is dead. He succeeds, however, in finding the true romance, the one touch of gold in that brief experience of crude bright alloys, and discovers that he and Ida Chatwick have miraculously fallen in love.

In the pattern of the story as well as the import of the moral *Wonder Hero* differs in no way from its three more impressive predecessors, and it has the fairy-tale atmosphere which Priestley exploited more seriously in *They Walk in the City*. He refers to Ida and Charlie as "these children of our industrial civilisation", but they are never, like Rose and Edward of the later book, swamped by the mechanics and harsh conspiracies of the age in which they live. Charlie is more sensible, more independent of mind and less respectful than Edward; the real point, however, is that Priestley has not yet reached that state of social concern which forced him to speak out so loudly in the later book. It is as though in the earlier novels his imagination was triumphantly suppressing a political demon which required for its release only a slight relaxation of Priestley's interest in character and situation for their own sake; and now already in *Wonder Hero* that process is to be observed, even though the tone is sardonic and the impulse chiefly to entertain. We are on

Charlie's side all the way but not because he is a person; although he is slickly characterised, his appeal rests on the fact that he is a figure pushed into inflated man-made circumstances of inordinate stupidity and yet managing to defy them with common sense. Ida too is no more than a doll whom we regard with warmth because we care for what she represents; and the rest of the people, as they should be, are as dry and flat as biscuits.

One's feeling is that Priestley has taken less trouble with imagining this book on a deeper creative level partly because he rightly realised that the story was too lightweight to be effective unless lightly and swiftly told, partly because his mind was turning away from the novel as the premier means of interpreting what he wished to say. By writing *English Journey* in 1934, a book which describes the aftermath of economic depression throughout the country, he proved his ability to find attractive personal expression for his urgent concerns, without descending to journalism or disguising them in fiction. Now that his creative energies had found a home on the stage, he had no further need of the novel and for the next ten or fifteen years he never seriously returned to it, except in *They Walk in the City* when he was anxious to emphasise a point which had emerged from his social explorations and thinking but which could not be palatably demonstrated in any other form.

A SCARLET THREAD

They Walk in the City compares with *Angel Pavement* in length and the attitude behind it springs from the logical development in more explicit, social terms of the ideas Priestley was quietly exploring and more imaginatively interpreting in the earlier novel. Hardly to be regarded as a novel at all, *They Walk in the City* is an object lesson, a lecture with plenty of lantern-slides on the increasingly mechanical civilisation of the thirties, in which natural ordinary people could be lost for ever, to each other and to their own spirits, in the desert of brick, the cruel maelstrom of self-seeking. In the autumn of 1935 Priestley visited

America and after staying a short while in New York moved
west to Arizona where he and his family occupied a ranch.
When he arrived, his immediate task "was to find the right
setting, the most suitable scheme of action, the best manner of
narration, for what seemed to me an attractive and not unworthy idea. This was to take two simple young people, typical
specimens of the exploited and helpless class, to bring them
together, part them, bring them together again, in the fashion
of the oldest and simplest love stories, but to place them and
their little romance within a strong framework of social
criticism. The two youngsters would be symbolic figures rather
than solidly created characters." When I first came across these
sentences in *Midnight on the Desert*, they crystallised a certain
anxiety I had felt when reading the book to which they referred.
For they are not the words of a novelist. For the first time I could
see Priestley turning away from the sheer curiosity, the exuberance in the face of life, and moving towards a cooler and less
creative appraisal of contemporary problems, social anomalies.
The imagination no longer seemed to be an end in itself, but a
means of supporting theories and ideas.

It is dangerous to begin a novel with the desire to prove a
point, for when the imagination is confronted with a force as
penetrating and indestructible as the intellect, it is liable either
to retreat in panic or make a squabbling unsatisfactory marriage. The first impulse of the creative writer must be to portray
life; if he wishes to expose it, he will show it up in a much more
incisive and telling fashion if he places the reader in the role of
an absorber—of atmospheres, implicit attitudes, points of view
concealed beneath a phrase—rather than in the position of a
listener, dispassionately weighing arguments and working
entirely through the mind. This was generally Shaw's method,
and in the eyes of immediate posterity, no longer shocked or
rattled by the adroit cocking of intellectual snooks, it has
already betrayed him; only a diamond brilliance of expression
has saved him so far, for the characters have none of the tenderness or depth that would keep them alive beyond their time.
Priestley's Rose and Edward in *They Walk in the City* are

handled with tenderness and make an impression of charm but they lack depth, and in this respect they have much in common with the fairy-tale figures who hurry through frightened forests or are immured in the castles of ogres. This, certainly, is the effect Priestley intended to give; indeed, his practised skill enabled him to carry out exactly what he had in mind, to make a just disposition of the various balances within the book.

The trouble is that one doubts whether these balances are acceptable *in toto*. Anyone coming to this book, whatever he happens to be looking for, will be disappointed in one aspect or another, so that the total effect—all that matters from Priestley's point of view—will be lost on him. Each of these aspects, such as situation, character, descriptive evocation, narrative, reflection, is developed precisely to the point at which it becomes useful to the book's general purpose, it is kept in control and never given its head. It is true that descriptions often spread abundantly through the chapters but they are geared to a debating-point and the rich physical colour drains out of them. Only at the beginning, when they are slowly shaping into characters and forming the bond of love which will enable the book to proceed in its plan, are Rose and Edward permitted to occupy the central position without much comment from the author; thereafter they recede, because the author's voice is too loud for them. This is the first book in which Priestley appears to have deliberately repressed his creative energy to allow the politician and social thinker to crowd the forefront of his mind and shout themselves hoarse. Neither subtle nor commanding as a novel, this is the work of a serious artist putting himself directly in the service of his time.

The narrative is always subdued to the moral, and for that reason, however successful Priestley's efforts to bring it in line with probability, it never manages to be finally convincing; not because it lacks verisimilitude in itself but because the reader senses the real reason why things are happening as they are. Narrative quite rightly objects to being put into chains for any other purpose than telling a story. Yorkshire once again begins this book: Edward and Rose, pleasant unaffected products of the working class, live in Haliford and chance to meet one halcyon moorland afternoon. Priestley's gentle account of their hesitations and spurts towards intimacy over an enormous tea establishes the warmest promise for the novel, and the couple arrange to meet again. But the kind of coincidence intervenes which everyone always fears and no one quite believes in, when Edward locks himself inescapably in the bathroom as he prepares to go and meet Rose. They miss each other, and immediately afterwards in her disappointment Rose leaves for London with a girl-friend and becomes a waitress with lodgings in Islington. Edward desperately follows her, and for the rest of the book the two of them are in London, never meeting, always searching, lonely and frightened, baulked at every turn by the monster city in whose crawling entrails they live. Once they succeed in meeting, during a political riot in Trafalgar Square, but Rose who is injured and loses Edward in the crowds, falls into the clutches of a strange exotic woman who arranges pretty dates for high-level customers.

At this point melodrama rather oddly and refreshingly forces its way into the story, which gathers pace towards a violent and unsavoury climax; Edward, sweeping in like the timely lover of legend, at last rescues his beloved from the sexual degradation into which she is about to be pushed by her patroness. The end of the book, where we find these simple and uprooted wanderers falling at last into each other's arms and apparently unhurt by their experiences, is suddenly very moving indeed; it was inevitable that Priestley should allow the human beings to have the last word but for most of the time they have been so rigorously kept under their author's moral indignation at the way circumstances are treating them that their final reunion comes with an effect of surprise.

In one way *They Walk in the City* was Priestley's most ambitious performance to date, for he was compelled to sacrifice or at least control several skills he had proved in his previous work. Well-realised individuals, unique but still typical, of the kind which carry the action in both *The Good Companions* and *Angel Pavement* would have reacted sufficiently violently against the terms in which this book was conceived to destroy its effect. That is not to say that real people would invalidate Priestley's argument and that therefore the book bears no relation to life at all. It is merely that we are all so committed to the short sight of our own inevitably narrow lives and cannot in a moment see the immense scale of cause and effect in the composition of an industrial society that it requires to be presented in an extreme and simplified form in order to be seen at all. Priestley, to make his thesis clear in detail as well as harsh in impact, is taking examples, and they are bound to be simple ones. The social scene is surveyed no less rangingly than in *Angel Pavement*, but the people are kept to one side so that the links in the tangle of chains can be seen and the dangerous clankings heard, so that we are aware in detail of what an individual person has to face when he accepts the values of urban civilisation and tries to live in accordance with them.

Rose and Edward are pleasant but colourless; the people picked out of the masses surrounding them cannot indulge the reader in savouring their personalities, for they are present only to play the formal part required of them; we know, for example, that the earnest dramatist Rose serves in the café is only there with a view to warning her that if you "turn down the wrong street, you're lost for ever", and he is less attractive for that. Priestley also seems to be voluntarily thwarting his urge to record scenes and atmospheres with his dispassionate reliable eye in favour of giving them the purely intellectual slant his purpose needs, and though they are still true to his nature, they lack the power and depth of some of his earlier description. There is still strong feeling in the way he describes London, but the feeling has been intellectualised, it is hard and angry, and therefore makes a less forceful appeal to the emotions. At the beginning of chapter seven we may be stirred by his grand dejected sweeping of the eye across the wastes of Greater London, for it is a statement of fact presented by a controlled and bitter eloquence; we are not, however, moved by it. For this reason Priestley was accused of mere reporting in this book, and if this is not strictly fair, at least it suggests that he is presenting facts rather than impressions and building his intellectual conclusions into those facts. Nobody likes this much; we feel we are being assaulted by a point of view that will brook no argument.

Once again realism and romance are present, but this time they are in conflict, fighting each other tooth and nail, as though Priestley, growing into a more serious view of his responsibilities, no longer believed that they were capable of reconciliation. In our present society harmony is impossible on a social level but still to be struggled for on the personal. James Agate wrote that "the realist in me insists that this is the worst great book I have ever read, the romantic that it is the best bad book I know", and it is hard not to share that feeling of worthwhile failure, of positive and valuable creative forces being cramped and given the wrong forms. The conception is vitally important and Priestley is watching his world from a much loftier eminence than ever before; the energy of the book was poured into the sweep and detachment of the observation, into the establishing of a consistent standpoint. But the book has been worked out and not naturally imagined, and intellectual energy alone is not sufficient to integrate its parts into an irresistibly persuasive pattern. I remember at the time of reading it that I was delighted by the story, and only afterwards when the book fell into its true shape in my mind, was I aware that it sagged and bulged here and there and had remained with me more as a *tour de force* than as a piece of living literature. Perhaps I should never have asked more from it than that first childlike pleasure in the way the story had been so neatly fitted together, in the simplicity of the people, the white faces of the innocents and the black hearts of the villainous and the shadowy forms of the anxious flitting in between. It is a fairy-story; Priestley asks no more for it.

However much was asked, even less was obtained for the rest of the novels which Priestley wrote over the next ten years. For *The Doomsday Men, Let the People Sing* and two novels written during the war, *Blackout in Gretley* and *Daylight on*

Saturday do not compare at all favourably with the fiction Priestley produced before he turned his inner eye towards Shaftesbury Avenue and his outward glance across the troubled face of this country. *Wonder Hero* gives one the impression that, though his mood is cheerful and he genuinely wants to tell a story in the old way, his foot is really on the bottom step of the rostrum and he is already rustling the angry papers in his hand. And when, in *They Walk in the City*, he is to be seen standing firmly in front of us in his own person, we are certain of it: to get the best out of Priestley during the next few years we must pull ourselves out of the armchair, put on a slightly better suit and telephone for a taxi. For we are going to the theatre.

VI. A Leading Playwright of the Thirties

THAT MAD OLD WITCH, THE THEATRE

I WAS not, however, in the theatre in 1932 when Priestley started working there; I was in the pram. My regular theatre-going did not begin until some years after the war, with the result that I am bound to approach the bulk and possibly the best of his dramatic work with only two guides to assist me: the first a strong visual imagination capable of putting quite a lively production of a play on the stage of the mind, the second, other people's recollections of the impact of certain plays when they were first produced. Both these guides are helpful, neither of them finally reliable, but as this is the principle on which an informal work of criticism should be based, the effort to stimulate interest rather than to dominate opinion, then perhaps one can make a certain amount of capital out of being born years too late to catch the effect of so many first nights in the context of their time.

Priestley's plays, though not always naturalistic, are never anything but natural in the sense that they depend entirely on performance for their effect. The words do not matter except as a vehicle for the character speaking them and as a means of forwarding the action. Spasms of poetry, of music in the phrase, are rare, and Priestley has difficulty in writing them because a touch of the rhetorical often intrudes between his emotion and the delicate poetic nerve he sometimes strives to reach. In stage dialogue, too, it is hard to suggest a rounded individual character unless the words are spoken aloud; printed on the page they are merely the foundation for the performance. Dialogue in fiction, even when it is totally realistic, errs towards exaggeration and is supported by the novelist's choice of frame for every remark: he asserted, he equably agreed, he said— these asides of narrative fill out the character. One suspects that dramatic dialogue which gives everything to the reader and destroys his need to see the play is always difficult and sometimes impossible to act.

This, however, is not so with Priestley. There is nothing in his plays which cannot and should not be picked up even as it is spoken in the theatre. In some ways I think it a pity that a reading edition of these plays is available. They should more properly be found between the tattered blue paper-covers of acting editions, the various parts underscored in red by small-town amateurs who once performed the play, for the piece then seems immersed in the theatre, surrounded by the faint echoes of former and future productions, and as close to the stage as a mere book can come. But to put plays between hard boards and issue them in a public edition is to advance them as works of prose literature, and this they can never be except in the act of performance. For in Priestley's work characters and situations are fulfilled artistically only when expressed and developed by actors. This is not to say that his interest in the theatre, like that of Terence Rattigan, is confined exclusively to character, situation and a neat plot to exploit them. George Calderon declared the Russian drama to be centrifugal rather than centripetal, the object being to lift the audience's attention from particular events to a general contemplation of life rather than to focus interest narrowly on a group of individuals, and in this sense Priestley is closer to the Russians than most English playwrights of the last thirty years. It makes his plays better worth reading than the momentary fizz of cleverness, the transient pieces that paradoxically seem to make the longest runs in the contemporary theatre, but it does not drown their cry to be staged and seen.

A quintet of plays composed in the thirties form the centre piece of his pre-war reputation, and they all either broach a theory of time or use the strangeness of time to give a twist to the action. Priestley plainly does not care very much whether you believe such notions or not; he is not trying primarily to arrest his audience and turn them into disciples. Priestley has suffered since the early thirties from having pulpits and platforms piled at his door even when he is not preaching, and it is a grave error to judge him in the first place on the principles he drew out of the thought of men like Ouspensky and J. W. Dunne to furnish his plays with a fresh and dramatic angle on the human scene. Moods and feelings concern him; atmospheres set his creative fingers drumming: to call him a dramatist of ideas crushes much of the breath out of his plays. For the purpose of selecting these provocations, these philosophical challenges, is to make the plays muscular, free to leap easily and unselfconsciously into those parts of people's lives where secrets are kept close, so that the most private words may be spoken at the most dramatic moments. Thus, on account of a premonition, a sense of time mysteriously twisting her round its finger, Janet Ormund in *I Have Been Here Before* can conquer her reserve in a moment before a perfect stranger. Any theory to which Priestley appears to be giving his support in these early plays has been examined by him, not for its inherent interest and probability, but entirely for its dramatic value, for the assistance it can give in extending the range and improving the depth of his power to convey the feelings and moods, so tenuous as to be virtually imperceptible on the naturalistic stage, which appear to him essential reflections of the way humans live.

Obviously, as Priestley explains in *Midnight on the Desert*, these theories absorbed him philosophically for a time as well. But any explanation of them in the text, as when Alan in *Time and the Conways* explains to his sister Kay the idea that at any one moment we are only a cross-section of our real selves, is provided, not to sharpen the point of a notion that Priestley is determined to get across, but to make quite certain that we are weighing these passages of human activity in the very balance the dramatist intends. If we are not aware of this particular point that time does not destroy but preserves, then the dramatic irony of the third act is merely tasty, a savoury to

smack the lips over. There is none of the satisfaction of that
haunting true irony that imprisons the play's mood in the mind
after the curtain has swished down, so that we find it unexpectedly incorporated in our complex fashion of looking at
other people and ourselves. *Time and the Conways* contains a
simultaneous vision of a long view of certain individual lives
and the trivial momentary details within them, as though one
could read close print and survey a landscape at the same
second.

Writing for the stage very quickly became for Priestley an
opportunity to move inwards, to escape from the busy society
of his novels and regain the private room from which the earlier
essays and criticisms had been written. His concern had always
been with character, but the view we have of the people in his
fiction tends to be distant and external; they are shown and
spoken for, their deeper feelings are assumed rather than
naturally revealed, except when a glimpse becomes necessary
for the forwarding of the total machine. Society, displayed as
an intricate and chaotic apparatus of eccentric cogs, as unpredictable as a cartoon engine, seemed to be more important
than the people who composed it. For Priestley the excitement
of the conception lay in its breadth and scope, in creating a
full society, in sweeping an alert extrovert eye across a thickly-
peopled landscape. The depth of the conception was never
firmly present in the execution of these books, for it depended
on that sympathy of mind which makes an author's observations
cut deeper with certain readers than the actual meaning they
contain. This is not to suggest that Priestley's novels are
littered with subtleties available only to readers who approach
him in a state of peculiar refinement: books are picked up and
thrown down by anyone who cares to look at them, not made
an object of quiet preparatory meditation. But if a rounded
character at any level makes an impact, from Scobie in *The
Heart of the Matter* to Jess Oakroyd in *The Good Companions*, one
may be sure that the author knows much more about him than
he needs for his purpose to tell us, and something of this
knowledge, lying just under the words and striking deep, will

float as an atmosphere of personality into our perception of that character. In fact he takes possession of us, and without thinking we know how he would feel if he happened to be here at this moment.

The plays, however, do not overlook society from a high window, picking out people here and there for special mention. They start inside people and they are about life as individuals see it, in close-up, confined to rooms, devoted to the urgencies of detail and the intensities of feeling. Priestley does not neglect the world in which these groups of people spend their narrow tightly-clenched days, for it is one of his virtues as an artist that he always sets his detailed scene in a neatly sketched background and one of the sources of his popularity that these backgrounds are immediately recognisable and sympathetic to his audiences. But he is concerned now with the world inside and he is writing from within, seeing and showing the outward world in terms of the people he sets moving in it. His plays rarely demand that we should confine our sympathies to one or two characters. All the people are so shaped and tilted towards the audience that it is impossible not to see and feel the situation in which they are all engaged from all their points of view.

This perhaps implies a diffusion of interest that does not actually exist, for Priestley holds the piece together by varnishing the surface with his own attitude towards the matter, his own conception of the realities with which his people are dealing. In *Time and the Conways* he lights the situation from an unusual angle without in any way casting false shadows across the faces on the stage and his attitude is apparent in Alan's speech to Kay which I have already quoted. But although the human issues which the family are fighting out within the play could exist without reference to any conception of time, they are not dissociated from the mood of melancholy optimism which this particular theory generates in the mind. Priestley has not, as one critic suggested, merely reversed the order of the second and third acts. The people have created the mood of the play spontaneously, the atmosphere issues from the pattern their temperaments weave, and this mood turns the

I

mind sadly towards the passage of time, the transience and pathos of all things human. All human relationships have a particular mood which is often a more reliable guide to their spirit than any words the people involved may speak or any actions they take. *Eden End* is a play which, superficially somewhat flat and ordinary in its concerns, proves to be an alchemical mixture of such moods, providing undertones to a series of domestic dramas and giving them both movement and the power to move.

Jung, who believed that the artist should strike a balance between the inward and the outward eye so that he could contrive to look both ways at once, told Priestley once that he thus combined the extrovert and introvert in his work to an almost perfect degree. Such a lavish testimonial does not appear to affect him in the writing of novels, but in Priestley's best plays the balance is precise, and even in the doubtful pieces he is led astray, not so much by the focus of vision in which the thing was conceived, but by a habit of mind which often at the last moment sacrifices the truth to a rather hazy idealism that climbs by way of rhetoric into a blue-sky sentimentality. The last act of *Johnson Over Jordan* is injured, though perhaps not fatally, by this sort of wishful-thinking. It is as though Priestley felt that by calling in a few sweet words, a pill of reality would be sugared; instead it turns sourer. But the sentimentality is not always due to this. Occasionally it results from Priestley's attempt to balance on that exquisite edge of emotion, the eye unexpectedly turning inwards from the noisy world and speaking in a hushed voice of the vague discoveries it makes there; an attempt which is sometimes banal, even excruciating, but occasionally moves the audience intensely. In order to succeed at all, an artist must always travel close to the brink of failure.

THE SPEED OF AN EASY LETTER

Dangerous Corner, the first of the plays, was written in 1932 and produced at the Lyric Theatre in the early summer of that year. The play has been performed often and everywhere since, in every kind of theatre up and down the country, and it has made long journeys to all parts of the world. Sixteen years after its first performance, for its inclusion in the collected plays, Priestley wrote: "It has never been a favourite of mine, for it seems to me merely an ingenious box of tricks, which I constructed to prove I could think and create like a dramatist and not necessarily like a novelist, and also to make use of the device of splitting time into two, thus showing what *might* have happened, an idea that has always fascinated me." Priestley proved his point. At least no critic could say that he was trying to cram novels into the narrower confines of the stage, however little they liked the work from other points of view. For James Agate was almost alone in his unrestrained praise of the piece, although a later revival at the Westminster in 1937 managed to persuade the same bunch of critics to reverse their opinion entirely, as though the intervening years had given the piece time to mature.

The play has seven characters of whom one, a lady novelist, is confined to two brief appearances; the other six are all concerned in the firm that publishes her books and most of them are related. Here they are at the beginning, regarded by society as a sweet, lucky and well-established set and even seeming to themselves, by a refusal ever to admit the truth, just "nice easy-going people". But the facts are very different; the facts are ugly. The women have been listening to a radio play after dinner, in which the husband kills himself after unearthing some disagreeable family secrets. When the men join the ladies, they all briefly worry the point that truth is a sleeping dog and then, very naturally, the conversation takes one turn where it might with equal ease have taken another. The death of an attractive and quixotic brother who died by his own hand six months before slips like a ghost into the talk and proceeds to rattle all the skeletons that have been lying at their ease in the cupboards for so long. One of them, ingenuous in his anxiety for the truth, persists in questioning them all so intensely that by the end of the evening every shred of decency has been stripped off them all and they are skeletons too. But, like Samson, he finds he has brought crashing round his head the temple of this so cosy well-favoured society, and there is no choice but to die. As he shoots himself the action returns to the moment when the husband in the radio play pulls the trigger, and once again they sit there discussing it until the dangerous corner has been passed and they seem all set to chat idly for the remainder of the evening.

After the first night in 1932, Agate wrote: "If this is not a brilliant device, I do not grasp the meaning of either word, and if the plot is not a piece of sustained ingenuity of the highest technical accomplishment, I am not an impercipient donkey but an ass who has perceived too much." A brilliant device it certainly is, but it is no more than that for it does not colour the audience's view of the whole action of the play; only in the denouement comes the rushing awareness of the point of this ingenuity, and then it is too late for Priestley to convey anything more valuable than a sudden powerful feeling of the strangeness of life, of the softness of the ground we tread and of the way we forget how fatal the most trivial of our daily actions can be. This, one might think, is enough for any play, but it is better theatre than philosophy. At the end of the piece the effect is of shock, a release of tension that satisfies an audience which has been concentrating on the story, but it does not provoke thought of sufficient depth to send people away with any more lasting legacy than a sense of good entertainment. Priestley's tale is too absorbing in itself. In the convolutions of the plot lies the secret of both the success and the failure of the play. Only when a dramatist deliberately gives one pause, when in fact he interferes with the smooth development of his story, shakes the audience out of its concentration and then pulls it roughly back, only then does he make room for any deeper meanings he may have to offer. It has always been one of Priestley's faults that by making it too easy for others, he had made it difficult for himself.

The merits of the play's construction are obvious and have always been the first concern of anyone who wrote about it. The effect of a good construction on the mind in any branch of art is to give it a spring-clean, to make it orderly and to reject from it anything irrelevant to what is being said within the construction; it concentrates the attention. However unsophisticated an audience in the ways of art, it will always be irritated by lack of tidiness, by loose ends and by the abrupt inconclusive pauses which we know exist in life but which are a mild, if sometimes rewarding source of annoyance in art. A tidy room, however, has its limitations. There is something clean and expressionless about it which seems to inhibit rather than lubricate the flow of emotion.

But we can speak too much about construction, a matter of far greater significance in the plastic arts than in literature, even than in the drama; we can never talk enough about the smallest things a writer says, or fails to say, or implies. In plays of what Priestley himself calls "apparent naturalism", much can be said which either may be missed altogether by the audience or can jog the mind into thought when it is least expecting it. In pure naturalism no imagination is needed on the part of the audience, but in Priestley's type the imagination is called upon to add, if not a dimension, at least a perspective to the world, based on the implications of the piece. *Dangerous Corner* is closer to apparent naturalism than Priestley's next serious play, *Eden End*, and further from it than most of the plays that followed in the thirties, but this is not plain until the end and we probably tend in watching it, as we have said, to take it at its face value. There is nothing wrong in this: Priestley always intends his work to be taken at its face value, without any undue effort on the part of reader or audience, and he designs his work to show as much of its character as possible on its face. It is often his own fault if he is accused of superficiality.

For me *Dangerous Corner* makes one point that lies very close to reality. It shows how capable people are of abiding quite serenely by the rules of civilised conduct, even in the swirling undercurrents of their private lives, first of all without any particular discontent (though on the edge of profound unhappiness all the time), but more important, without being truly aware of the pitch of falsehood to which their lives have sunk. The mental dishonesty on which the play depends has no meaning in itself for the characters; they have formed the habit of taking its dictates for the truth. Robert Caplan could have taken and made the best of all the confessions sprung upon him during the evening of *Dangerous Corner* if only they had come frankly to his ears before the first falsehood was uttered or the first opportunity for truth allowed to slip past. But we can never forgive people who poison the past for us by showing us quite how foolishly we have been deceived; it touches a vanity of such depth that we are ready to kill or die for it.

The other comment which *Dangerous Corner* prompts one to make on the subject of truth is that once more, this time where human relations are concerned, there is no absolute. By rigidly adhering to the truth as we see it, we present the matter in question in an entirely different light from someone else whose particular truth, or standard of truth, may be dependent on emotional circumstances that have nothing in common with our own. A man in love sees one truth about the situation of love; the woman not in love with him sees another. If the woman deceives him he alone views it as deceit, while she truly is quite free from it, both in intention and in a moral sense. In this case one may say that the people in *Dangerous Corner* are all acting in accordance with their own individual notions of the truth, to avoid hurting others and causing upsets; but this is not so, for they are each conscious of guilt and that destroys all awareness of truth. It is important that writers should continually command us to act fearlessly and without indolence, for one of the first tasks in searching for a higher truth is to wriggle out of their fear and to renounce the idleness into which they commonly fall. If Priestley had been more fearful, he might have succeeded in offending fewer people by his work; if he had succumbed occasionally to laziness, he could doubtless have produced a less uneven flow of writing. These seem small advantages beside what he has gained in a personal search for the truth.

THE CURIOUS HAUNTING

For the past seven years, early each September, string quartets have been performed in the lofty hall of Priestley's house in the Isle of Wight, and there are three days when the undercurrent of musical interest in his life bursts to the surface, an audience comes, and one is reminded of those unexpected but passionate encounters with music that occur from time to time in his work. Virginia Woolf's prose often suggests that she might have written with a Mozart quartet ringing in her ears, and in Henry James the orchestration, abstract and impressive, moves as heavily as a symphonic development in Vaughan Williams. But with Priestley the prose contains a rhythm but no music, like a subtle form of drumming, and that is why his personal absorption in the art of music is unexpected when evidence of its strength slides into a book or play. One of the set-pieces in *Angel Pavement* is the vigorous imaginative effect of a Brahms symphony on the untutored ears of Mr. Smeeth, the undulating autumnal melodies of Elgar's cello concerto weave significantly in and out of the action of *The Linden Tree*, *Johnson Over Jordan* was conceived with music an essential part of it (Benjamin Britten provided the score), and of course *Music at Night* is entirely based on the impact music makes on various types of mind and the natural candid blossoming of people under its spell.

One feels that the time-plays, as gently as smoke, drifted out of a mood which might have been served with finer satisfaction if Priestley had been, not a writer of plays, but a composer of music; for they belong to exploration on those levels where words are often an embarrassment, where the logic of language is always getting awkwardly in the way and demanding further explanations whenever it attempts to explain something. Mood and feeling in music require no defence and a composer need never be called to account for the ideas which his work may be thought to put forward, for he is delving in a pure inexplicable art in which the statement is absolute and only emotional acceptance need be found for it. But when a mood is cast delicately into the form of a literary idea, the heart may be willing to succumb to its climate while the mind is perplexed, possibly irritated and even alienated by it. Art can rarely make a complete conquest of a mental objection on the part of the reader to a metaphysical argument propounded by the writer, and yet it is essential to win intellectual sympathy if the appeal to the emotions through the mood of the piece is to avoid being found too vague and woolly for effect.

This was one of the major problems Priestley faced when he was trying to reconcile his excursions into the nature of time and the reality of dreams with the solid wooden boards of the naturalistic stage on which he was still determined to stand. The problem has never been perfectly solved, but the instinct has always remained with him to lock up the logical objections in a cupboard of the mind, kill off the sneering doubts that cling to any notion that cannot immediately be proved, and set out on a few days of speculation, as much mood as thought, as though it were a walking tour through countrysides that might long ago have formed part of a dream. But this was never a holiday. "Every few years," wrote Priestley recently, "I feel compelled to vanish into the mazes of the Time problem, returning, rather worn, with a play or a story. . . . My interest in the Time riddle is part intellectual, part intuitive. I am intellectually curious, like a man faced with some half-deciphered hieroglyphics, and am pricked on, as such a man might be, by an intuitive feeling that here is the great challenge." It may be true, as he suggests, that there is no particular emotional drive behind this adventuring; Priestley is not fearfully fighting his way back to a past where the people glowed like angels and the skies were bluer than heaven. Most of us gild the past, not because we want to return to it, but because it belongs to us totally like a loved one who died in our arms, and Priestley, who must have begun more sentences with such words as "when I was a boy in the North" than any but the most persistent of ageing clubland nostalgics, only employs the past emotionally in his work to expand the present—though he may sometimes use the former intellectually and in social debate to belittle the latter.

But for all that the force that pushes him into the dim corridors of time is still an emotional one; or, if that is not strictly true, the effect is emotional in the sense that he is moved by his reflections, his heart is touched by the spectacle of people involved in the dilemma of time. His time plays are not trying to solve a problem but to see it more clearly, to wrest from the quick unusual glimpse no cheering token that a promised land exists but a proof that the promised land is here and now, then and there, ensuring the future and preserving the past, if only we will take the trouble to pause for a moment and look for it. "It has never been suggested," Priestley wrote, "by any of us time-theorists that a little fiddling with the clock will put all right for us. We have never suggested that there is an easy way out. It is in fact precisely this view that we challenge." Priestley may sometimes be accused of dispensing comfort too lavishly, not offering it with honesty as the drug his readers instinctively feel it to be, but putting it forward as a genuine sweet essence distilled from an elysian flower. In moments of vitality one often commits the folly of mistaking a glandular condition for a moment of visionary truth, and that serious and challenging play, *They Came to a City*, does suffer a little in this way.

But despite this Priestley is not trying to make it easy. He is— quite a different thing—looking for ways of making it less difficult and succeeding, as always in exploration, in discovering more and more problems along the way. In the ventilation of such problems lies the value of Priestley's serious plays. The surface of them chatters with dramatic argument, moves neatly with people working out a well-constructed plot. Sometimes, as in *I Have Been Here Before*, the plot is directly concerned with the discoveries Priestley is airing, the undercurrents rise close to the surface and break into the action, taking it out of human hands so that we watch people behaving under haunting unknowable influences. In *Time and the Conways*, as we have seen, the pressures of mood that give the play its character only once break surface and become a matter for open discussion on the stage. But how they are exploited technically is hardly important; their dramatic purpose is to generate a mood, to display human lives in an atmosphere infrequently if ever evoked, and thus to murmur something scarcely audible about human life itself.

A SPECIAL TENDERNESS

Dangerous Corner uses time only for the planting of a device, a piece of business; its true business rests elsewhere. Priestley's next serious play, *Eden End*, came in 1924 and it was produced at the Duchess Theatre in the autumn. The action of this piece was taken back to 1912, not, as James Agate wrote, "for the easy irony of the 'good time coming', but because of the greater poignancy of that passing moment which has all the illusion of urgent life and that we know to be in yesterday's grave." So now time is merely a presence, an almost unbearable secret passed between Priestley and his audience but not a true breathing of the play. Possibly it provides an eminence from which we see the chaos of lives in relation to the pattern of life, the disappointments and wrong turnings still doing their best to keep the ideal in view. In a sense we are on the same ground as *Time and the Conways*. The mood is not tragic because the issues are as gentle as those that affect our own lives and we never, except in moments of self-pity or megalomania, view ourselves as figures of tragedy; it is touched by a quiet melancholy that stills the atmosphere to the point of tears, despite Wilfred's rag-time gramophone and the tense battles of words that burst into the mild domestic scenery.

There is something in this play, a quality in the air of it that the first moments establish, that I find hard to suggest—for it is delicate and easily to be dismissed as illusory—and Priestley, even if he tried, never found a play to capture it again. One can say, not very helpfully, that it was his closest approach to Chekhov, particularly to that silence, first broken by diminishing cries and then total and devastating, that comes almost at the end of *The Cherry Orchard*. And one can mention the terrible silence that falls on the theatre, as well as on the stage, when the Professor in *The Linden Tree* raises his finger in the midst of a family dispute and asks them to listen to the sounds from upstairs of Dinah practising her cello. This is the variety of sadness, not at all sentimental, seemingly a long way from human affairs but actually close to the essence of them, as vague and distant and old as the man who enters to break that silence in Chekhov, yet belonging so intimately to the present moment, that *Eden End* somehow distils from material that is neither profound nor original nor especially beautiful in itself. But a beautiful play has been made.

The critic William Archer said of a play by Ibsen that "he simply took a cutting from the tree of life, and, planting it in the rich soil of his imagination, let it ramify and burgeon as it would", and one has this feeling of a natural process moving without interruption to a predestined goal about *Eden End*. It is no use asking what *Eden End* is about or demanding to know the point of it; in the course of it, if a sensitive production wins your sympathy, the subject and conclusion will make themselves felt, stealing over you as suddenly as a wind shivering in the trees and just as surely rejecting words in the effort to describe it. This may sound an alarmingly elaborate way of sidetracking critical responsibility towards what is, after all, a three-act play concerned with a Yorkshire doctor's family before the first war, but however remote Priestley seems from the icy northern passions of Ibsen and the touching inflections and insinuations of Chekhov, *Eden End* is still a play which words need to be softer of outline and more whispered in tone to convey.

Priestley himself has an unrivalled sense of words, but no great feeling for them, no instinctive awareness of the depths an individual word will plumb or the weight it will carry; for him, they are of the head without being heady. He is never stormed by them into that blind oblivious assurance which carry poets happily through unspeakable dangers. But the poetry is there, finding its outlet in the conception of the piece, even if it sometimes dies for want of words. It does not die in *Eden End*, however, and it is interesting that Priestley should have forgotten, with a faint sense of wonder, what caused him to write it: "everything in it is imagined, and I know nothing in my

own life that would suggest to me this particular theme of the
pathetic prodigal daughter." Why should he remember? One
finds it easier to accept the thought of a wayward visitation
when there is a quality in the piece which defies the effort to
pin it down.

It gave him great satisfaction to write this play, and there
was certainly one fact he could remember: "the exquisite
summer evening when I completed the last act, the tender light
of the dying day on my last page." Whatever the motive,
pushing the ideas which charge the piece so far away from you
that they can only be felt and no longer seen and heard, the
only sure way of establishing three acts firm and perfect was to
begin with the characters, end with them and live intensely in
their presence throughout. One must contrive the kind of
relationship, deep but relaxed, that only flourishes when you
can give yourself time for it. It is true that characters in a novel
cannot be spun out of a hasty acquaintanceship. In a form
which, more like life, shapes its action and ropes in its outlying
places as it moves forward, often racing beyond the novelist's
intention and taking amazing turns under his very eyes, the
characters can afford to be flexibly known before the first page
is written, capable of developing according to the way they
strike each other as time goes on. This, however, is out of the
question within the tighter schedule of a play, where every
word a character speaks must be, if necessary, justifiable by
argument.

In his preface to *Eden End* Priestley wrote, "I brooded for a
long time over the people of this play and their lives, and then
wrote it quickly and easily; and to my mind this is the way
that plays ought to be written. The long brooding brings depth
and richness; and the quick writing compels the whole mind,
and not merely the front half of it, to work at the job." Perhaps
the success of *Eden End* was due to a pitch and quality of silence
that came to Priestley at a time when he most needed it.
Certainly, since he moved to live on the Isle of Wight in 1934
and could stare at wide downland with only the flicker of birds
to distract an attention wandering beyond the boundaries of

time, his opportunities for entering this close relationship with his characters must have improved. In the grim winter of 1947 when his house was short of fuel and blanketed with snow, he was forced to eat, work and sleep in one small room for ten days or so, and during that spell of exile he wrote *The Linden Tree*. It is hard to imagine any serious playwright preserving intact the consistency of his mood and thought through the cocktail gabbling, the shrilling of telephones, the ever-demanding voices that confront him in London. But at the west of the Isle of Wight the days are unselfconsciously longer, the horizons wider and a glimpse of the sea washing the southern cliffs is always full of reflections, not only of the sky, but of people and stories as well.

THE SPHINX'S RIDDLE

Dunne described his book, *An Experiment with Time*, as "the account of an extremely cautious reconnaissance in a rather novel direction". Like most people I skipped over the latter part of the book where he brings his precise mathematical training to bear on the philosophical belief he has already tried to prove empirically in the first chapters. The theory is too well known to require much description here; the mere mention of its author's name conjures it out of the air as instantaneously as a dream and nowadays we are apt to regard it avuncularly as an innocent game played madly in the thirties, with a notebook and pencil ready beside the bed and the recital of dreams driving the breakfast table behind its newspapers. But whether we accept its conclusions or not, this enquiry remains valid human experience; it may not succeed in finally answering any of the riddles of time, dreams and self-consciousness with which it is concerned, but it provides a philosophical attitude to them based on fallible but still legitimate experience.

Unfortunately attitudes which become the fashion grow whiskers very quickly and are packed off to hermitages out of harm's way, and for this reason many people today find that the play Priestley built out of the theory has become a little

tarnished with, ironically enough, the passing of time. Ideas
like this can be treated more seriously when they have been
disproved, when we can stop feeling sophisticated about them
and grow wise. These are the years when the fever of first
discovery has diminished and the fear that they may possibly
be true has not yet trailed away; it is reasonable to suggest
that *Time and the Conways* will eventually become a philosophical
period-piece as well as a quaint play of past manners. It is hard
to judge it now by purely literary standards, for the play is
slung half-way in time between the two periods of clearest
critical thinking, the moment of first arrival and the moment
of first dissociating it from its period, and today we are still
the hung-over victims of the poets and writers who drank
deeply of their ideas twenty or thirty years ago.

However, to summarise: within the fourth dimension, time
is the stationary object and we move about inside it. On a
journey from Piccadilly to Hyde Park Corner, if one pauses at
the Ritz for a moment's thought, one does not assume that
because Piccadilly has been left behind and Hyde Park Corner
is still to come, neither of them therefore exist. The rules that
thus apply to space are extended to time, for both belong to
the same logical pattern of the universe. Then, instead of
continuing one's way towards Hyde Park Corner, one must
imagine spending a night at the Ritz and dreaming, not only
that yesterday one smiled at a girl in Piccadilly wearing a
dress as blue as smoke, but also that you will tomorrow glimpse
a flash of red hair reflected in a taxi-window at Hyde Park
Corner and turn round to catch sight of someone you knew
well ten years ago. In dreams one moves freely in the new
dimension, and one has always smiled at the blue girl and
glimpsed the red hair, one is always going to meet these
experiences and one always *is* meeting them.

Although this theory has become as much a part of an
undergraduate's first-year equipment as a selection of bow-ties,
it is still possible to believe in it if one employs it scientifically
to expand the sense of mystery we feel in the presence of time,
rather than to explain the mystery away. Dunne was seriously

engaged in the pursuit of factual truth. Priestley, however, snatching the benefits of Dunne's method, takes off at once into the realms of thought suggested to his mind by the theory, examining them discursively, searching with care for suspicions of the mystical, trying to discover what other roots in our common experience are touched by such a notion, and above all, inevitably, surfacing with an urgent need to exploit the matter artistically.

This, in the autumn of 1937, produced *Time and the Conways*. It is plain that the problem of the Conways and people like them was a natural concern for Priestley. Belonging himself to their class, growing up among them at a time when the established order of society kept their values and attitudes strictly in joint, he had discovered with them after the first war that the social revolution, the busy changes afoot in the twenties, were going to knock them harder than anyone else. They were the buffer states, ears pricked to the growling either side of them and not knowing which way to turn. The middle class was cast adrift at that time and never since has it found an anchorage. Priestley has always been its voice, attempting to define a new position it can hold with the same solid strength as before, at the same time as he proposes means of assuaging the despair that visits individuals lost without clear principles and beliefs in the midst of a changing society. Such people are the Conways. The plan of the play first of all displays the happy coincidence that brought a temporary intellectual concern of Priestley's to the service of a permanent human one, the latter perhaps sharpened at that time by his survey of life after the economic crisis of the early thirties which appeared in *English Journey*. It was not a question of dredging up some human material suitable to be exploited in a time prank. The play also suggested that, even if no acceptable comfort could be derived from this particular belief, a mood of hope could still glowingly exist provided that a belief of some sort was held.

The Conways consist of a mother, four daughters and two sons, and the first act shows them in the unselfconscious gaiety of birthday charades in 1919, when the future held extravagant

promise for all the children—one to be a novelist, one to marry
wealth, another for big business, a fourth to launch her political
ideals into the new world. After an opening fuss of characters
changing in and out of grotesque bundles of clothing, the
characters slowly and very surely settle into the imagination
and take firm root. They are drawn with that skill which
almost immediately makes every word they say curiously
moving, as though we were observing through a keyhole the
entirely natural activities of people at home with themselves.
Nothing of dramatic note may be said to happen; we merely
discover what these people trust and believe is going to happen
in their lives, what treasures lie buried in their illimitable
future. Only one of the sons, a dullish municipal clerk, is already
established in his ways; the rest are on fire.

The second act takes place nineteen years later and the fires
have all burned out. One girl died before she had time for
disappointment; the novelist's ideals have borne fruit in a
disastrous affair and film-star interviews for a newspaper; the
keen Fabian has soured into a schoolmistress; and the boy is
still borrowing money for shady business enterprises and hurting
the girl he so brightly married. They bicker and snarl at each
other, tense with bitterness that the treasure should have fallen
apart in their hands. Only the pipe-sucking stay-at-home has
settled mildly into a corner of contentment and it is he who,
quoting Blake's "Joy and woe are woven fine", broaches very
quietly the idea that "our real selves are the whole stretches
of our lives; death is not the end but rather the beginning of
real life".

This might be the end of the play, but in the third act we
return to that party in 1919 where now every word is sharply
and unbearably salted by the most refined irony, touched with
a significance that makes the characters even less self-aware,
and therefore more vulnerable, than they were before. Because
the implications of the two previous acts cannot avoid committing the last act to predictable climaxes, the audience does
not expect to be held by surprises or twists in the action that
planted no earlier clues. On the contrary, the emotional

satisfaction lies in the fact that we know what will happen and must breathlessly wait for our knowledge to be confirmed, as though listening impatiently for certain exquisite changes of key or sweet progressions in a familiar passage of music. The inevitable in art, although we are guided to anticipate it, always comes as a shock.

Let us move away from time for a moment, for the Conways exist outside the philosophic mood which Priestley uses to enclose them in a more subtle eloquence than their speech could command. Each character is clearly defined, a full personality close enough to a common type to be readily accepted without much special explanation but still conveying that sense of the unique individual which alone convulses the sympathies of an audience into emotions. The triumph, however, which Priestley only repeats with the same unerring skill in *The Linden Tree*, rests in the portrayal of the awkward balances which, while they accumulate in effect to suggest the almost self-sufficient unity of temperaments that families show to the world, actually divide the members of the family into sharp quarrels, unsteady relationships, sudden illogical bursts of affection. One feels that the individuals must be rather less interesting when released from the close family atmosphere; and in *Bright Day*, when the Alington family glow as if they shared a common heart but kept a constant spark of opposition flaring in their minds, this is discovered to be partly true. The extent to which people depend on one another for their feeling of independence is a subtlety of human relations very difficult to convey in the theatre, and although *Time and the Conways* is a play about human isolation, about people driven away from each other towards a self they cannot come to terms with, the very fact that Priestley has enclosed it in a family atmosphere at a time of festivity improves the poignancy.

Priestley, who seemed at home in the theatre from the moment he entered it, has now unquestionably made his home there. For *Time and the Conways* is the first of his serious plays in which he moves more openly away from the naturalist tradition of the prose drama, striking off on his own, not content

K

with allowing the implications of human behaviour to speak for themselves in muffled whispers but, by setting the action within a philosophical framework, giving those implications a chance to speak more openly. The moralist, in fact, has now been granted the confidence to emerge into the plays, just as he was beginning to haunt the novels a few years earlier, and the measure of Priestley's superiority in the theatre lies perhaps in the finer subtlety with which he contrives the marriage between the realistic well-shaped slice of life and the opportunity for moral comment. The latter never interferes with the natural conduct of the former. Yet it draws the essential atmosphere into the open and unobtrusively provides the audience with the only possible way of interpreting what they are seeing. It is a small point that a fresh view of time could comfort the Conways out of their misery and disillusion; after all, only two of them are aware of the panacea's existence. The real point is that we arrive at the truth about the Conways and are moved by that truth because Priestley has set them within the particular pattern he chose. It was a dramatic choice.

BEWILDERED ENQUIRIES

I Have Been Here Before opened in London a month later in the autumn of 1937. It must have appeared that Priestley was behaving a shade naughtily: down in the Strand they were nightly mouthing words that carried one theory of time, while at the Royalty in Dean Street the same writer's dialogue was pressing points about the same subject which could only be regarded as contradictory. If you attended these plays two nights running and came away with a cloudy vision and an irritable fringe of question-marks round your mind, you could hardly be blamed. But of course one was not sitting in at lectures in philosophy and expecting a logical return for one's time; plush stalls exercise different standards from rows of wooden chairs. Consistency is demanded from a writer only in his refusal to be consistent, for the presence of recurring ideas in art, even if they are applied to different situations, fixes a clot in the artist's bloodstream which will eventually cause his death. Much that Priestley has written since the war has been impatiently pushed aside because the work embodied ideas and attitudes which had received exhaustive attention earlier. "For several years," wrote Priestley in 1937, "I had had a hunch that this problem of Time was the particular riddle that the Sphinx has set for this age of ours . . . and that if it could be solved there might follow a wonderful release and expansion of the human spirit." Delving into this complex of queries and contradictions, he came up with two plays (and a third later) that illustrated two sides to the problem. This was artistically in order.

I suspect that at the theatre it is more difficult to resist the philosophical spell, the spine-tingling but improbable thesis of *I Have Been Here Before*, because in this far from obvious play there is a flaw as obvious as the plot. The plot is a case of A meeting B and C not liking it. The flaw lies in Priestley's insistence on developing Ouspensky's very difficult theory to the point where he can draw moral conclusions from it, and these are so patently absurd, scrambling out of the end of the play like a lunatic on the run, that our disbelief is suspended no longer and the curtain that falls is one of cynical dissatisfaction. A theory like this, as in *Time and the Conways*, should flit through the play as lightly as a ghost, and then remain afterwards to haunt the mind and keep one intelligently awake at night. But in this case Priestley lays his own ghost, thus into the bargain weakening the flesh and blood he has created.

Despite this, the play is tense, absorbing and provocative. The trouble is that the ideas are so necessarily obtrusive that the characters are not brawny enough to bear their weight without assistance from someone whom Priestley first conceived as a supernatural being, afterwards settling for an exiled German professor with psychic powers. This suggests that the characters were modelled expressly to illustrate the theme, and though they are perfectly lively and true, they never draw our sympathies as surely as the Conways, they never move us. One understands their predicament without caring enough, even though its solution may go some way towards solving our own.

A is a stiff and handsome young headmaster who, in a remote moorland pub one summer week-end, meets B and has immediate rapport with her. She has fallen out of love with C, her rich and powerful husband who has drunk himself into a daze of asking tired terrible questions about the nature of life. Into the action comes an exiled German professor who is studying the problem of recurrence and believes quite rightly that he has come across an example of it; he is aware precisely how these people are going to behave, how unhappy they will be as a result of their behaviour, and he is determined to use all his powers of persuasion to make them act differently. In the first act the exposition is subtle and telling, and Priestley tensely establishes an atmosphere in which the odd glimpses through the opaque barrier of time which occasionally happen to all of us are very dramatically suggested, while the characters are left to make their own impression. Priestley has little time for them as people and is only concerned with the problems of experience that obsess them, and we therefore welcome them more defensively than usual as if we knew they were hollow. This emphasis is essential to the whole vitality of the piece which depends, not on the characters who are just good enough to survive any treatment at the moralist's wily hands, but on the accumulation of many small twists of improbability in the opening scenes. Janet, the wife, must feel convincingly that she has been here before; she must reveal that some force has drawn her close to the headmaster without even knowing it herself; the Professor's curious remarks about the situation must be delivered quite frankly, surprising the characters without offending the audience's sense of likelihood. Throughout this delicate process the people are brought to life, not naturally, but by the force of their circumstances, by the special atmosphere created for them to inhabit, and within such a circumscription the dramatic experience they offer is valid, if somewhat oblique. In fact, *I Have Been Here Before* represents the illustration of a primary theme first of all by means of a secondary theme, Ouspensky's whirligig of time, and only then by means of real people battling their way through a vortex of real problems. No wonder these people never quite manage to stand on their own feet.

The primary theme was stated by Priestley in his original introduction to the play: he wanted to propose "a kind of Everyman of my own generation" who after experiencing the "deep distrust of life felt by so many moderns" developed into the belief that "the universe was not hostile or indifferent to his deepest needs". If these were indeed the first unfolding impulses of the play, then Priestley might have been wiser to expand the notion polemically, to spread it over the pages of an argumentative book, for art is an egocentric master who requires always to be considered first. A self-aware principle or line of thought will generally shrivel or lose its driving force if it expects the creative spark to serve it, to set it dazzlingly alight. Priestley is too intelligent and detached a writer to remain unconscious of what he is really saying in his work, and that is perhaps one of the reasons why the highest achievement in art has always soared just out of his reach, to leave him with the consolation of such a perfect and flexible command of craft, that effects which should have been natural and stunning only manage, somewhat distantly, to seem these things. For complete truth to life, a writer must begin with life and only afterwards realise that by accident he has touched on the truth. And this is the trouble here: Priestley begins with an idea he feels to be true and then looks around for some aspects of life which clothe it warmly enough to let it out of doors without catching cold.

Priestley further complicates the issue by allowing the secondary theme, the theory of recurrence, to place his Everyman, the overworked and disillusioned tycoon, in an impossible and rather undignified position. The idea, briefly, is this. Time is not a straight line on which the events in our lives are ticked at intervals, but a circle opening at birth and closing at death which, though it may coincide with other times and other people purely by chance, is entirely personal to us. At death we enter the same circle again and make the journey again, living exactly as before, except that there exists a possibility of inward change, moral improvement or deterioration, movements of the heart. The failure sinks a little more each time round until his circle diminishes and dwindles to nothing; a few rare people, by paying more attention to their homework every time, eventually manage to turn the circle into a spiral and thus escape from their treadmill. One is reminded of the donkeys at Carisbrooke tramping round and round, seemingly dying a death with every revolution; and indeed, except in a purely philosophical realm where it can tell us something deep and valid about the life we live without being strictly applied to it, the theory has a somewhat asinine character.

The Professor is trying to prevent the tragedy—the tycoon committing suicide, the illicit couple escaping to a life that will turn out disastrously—which he knows has happened before; he is attempting to break the circles of these people who have been slogging tediously round the race-track an unthinkable number of times. He is in fact a moral force, but one feels that he exercises it more to prove his theory to himself than because he cares, with the mature divine wisdom that' such a figure might be expected to show, what happens to his subjects. By telling the couple how their love will perish in squalor, he destroys their impulse to run away together and sends the girl back to her no longer embittered Everyman. Tragedy has been averted certainly, but even if we feel that they are wiser, will they necessarily prove happier? Joy and woe may still, in some more normal chancy life where revelations are all a part of the mysterious game, be woven fine, but if the Professor's impulse-killing psychic machinery were to enjoy any widespread success, we should all be so busy letting our ignorant natural desires be shouted down by the visitations of better nature that we should cease taking decisions altogether and come to a halt. Within a play, unhappily, there is no holding the idea, however subtly you shuffle away from naturalism.

So what? I suddenly realised, when I emerged from my brooding about the play and saw how my objections had come full-circle, that I was somehow very little closer to what I wanted to say. Perhaps the value of the play was that it should be so readily picked to pieces; we sit up in our seats, angrily fire questions at it, shake our fist at a theory or ponder one of the many points that are raised. Priestley is sometimes one of those authors who are too irritating to tolerate but too troublesome and insidious to dismiss; impressed against one's will, one dithers through all the arguable criticisms only to find that one is just as impressed as when one started. This is often the case with his polemical articles, deliberately designed with their fistfuls of generalisations and transparent tricks of persuasion to rub a reader's mind the wrong way and set the blood of thought tingling again, but it happens too with *I Have Been Here Before*. One cannot help being interested; however much, for the sake of intellectual dignity, you pretend to wriggle in your seat, the attention is held throughout the piece and you go away from the theatre muttering comments that sound vaguely like threats, determined to have a look at Ouspensky and see what possible truth it contains, even if you stick at the first thirty pages.

A CHOICE OF ADVENTURES

The next two serious plays that concerned me were also experimental and may be regarded as the natural outcome of their predecessors. This is not to say that they are better plays—neither, in fact, remotely approached the success of the two time plays—but rather that they represent a development in Priestley which he was typically too impatient to wait before exploiting. The first is *Music at Night*, which was specially written for the Malvern Festival of 1938 and was subsequently, after considerable rewriting, the first play to appear on the London stage when the theatres re-opened after the panic of closing at the declaration of war. The second is *Johnson Over Jordan* which of all the plays seems to be the one that springs most readily into discussion when Priestley's name is mentioned controversially, as much a battle-ground of sore points as *The Good Companions*: and this play appeared at the New Theatre in February 1939. Both these plays seem much more satisfactory in theory than in practice, and that perhaps accounts for the mental excitement which blinded Priestley to their inadequacy as pieces of stagecraft. In each case, however, he became absorbed with the problems of the method he had chosen to the exclusion of sufficiently deep thought about the content, and the fact that the subject matter is too cursory for the weight of technique employed to present it is bound to make one concentrate more on the spectacle than on the implications of the piece.

This may seem too easily to write off these plays even before I have examined them, and that is unfair to Priestley, for both of them gripped my attention in a tighter clenched fist of interest than any that preceded them. *Johnson Over Jordan* contains isolated moments, peaks of vivid unexpected beauty, that are Priestley's closest approach to releasing in theatrical terms his own muffled poetic impulses. These are the moments that do justice to his original plans, as he brooded about the play during an immense and jostling lecture tour across America in the autumn of 1937; "it was a play in which an apparent phantasmagoria would, if all went well, be given a deep and very moving significance." All did not go quite well; perhaps he hurried it; perhaps the mood of the time, anxious, nervous, moving more swiftly every day towards an inevitable explosion, was too much out of sorts to pull Priestley away from its influences and into the sensitive areas of dream he needed to explore. And it is possible that this mood of the time inhibited his audiences too, made them impatient, when their lives were tossing on such stormy waters, of an attempt to find some of the calmer places. For *Johnson Over Jordan*, despite its patches of terror, is an almost too hopeful, too homespun play, a play that disintegrates out of the sharp black shadows of a powerfully imagined hell of dreams into the cosy and, yes, somewhat jolly sunlight of the last act.

Priestley has sometimes complained that his face is an inadequate and often misleading guide to the man within. A figure who once recognised him in an hotel wrote afterwards to say that he looked so morose and irritable that he had not dared approach him, yet at the time Priestley was enjoying a happy and carefree week of holiday with his children. And this is to some extent true of his talent. His outward gifts of expression and habits of thinking do not belong to the same character as the direction in which his innermost thoughts move and, still more, the way in which they are moved. The fund of poetry never finds its phrase and somehow glides away from any conception designed to contain it. The vision that prompted *Johnson Over Jordan*—and it is a grand one, as exactly rich in possibility as Priestley first saw it—passes into the upper levels of his mind which turn out to be too conscious and orderly, insufficiently linked to the subtle complexes below, to stand the strain. What emerges then is a vision transformed into a glittering, clever and sometimes very fine production number, with only a few shreds and hints of that original beauty showing through. Priestley has described himself as such an indolent man that only a hopelessly difficult technical challenge can drag him out of the armchair and seat him tensely at the desk, and there are signs in both these experimental plays that the need to pour his energies into the solution of superficial, but none the less intractable, difficulties has drawn him too far away from the levels that gave them birth. An inspiration will never take care of itself, but in an experienced craftsman the technique probably will.

The title almost insists that *Johnson Over Jordan* is a play about life after death, but Priestley quite definitely insists that we shall not regard it as such. Jordan takes us inescapably to the promised land; Bardo, however, is the real bridge between the improbable but familiar world where we are sitting and the unfamiliar viewpoint to which Priestley requires us to be transported. Bardo is the intermediate condition in which Tibetans believe themselves suspended after death, "a prolonged dream-like state, in what may be called the fourth dimension of space filled with hallucinatory visions directly resultant from the mental content of the percipient". We are to look back over our shoulder at the permanent existence and true values of what we have done in our lives. Priestley is hot on the trail of the moment of truth, and he throws into the pursuit all that he has learned about the nature of time and the quality of dreams. We are told nothing of death, except by implication and in that fine moment at the close of the play when Johnson hesitantly asks "Is it—a long way?" This is a moment so sensitive and so profoundly calm after the shuddering procession of images and scenelets that it manages to digest, even to make it moving, the fact that Johnson is still wearing a bowler-hat and carrying a bag as he walks away from the earthly life towards the constellations. It is in fact one of the few occasions in the play when the hero makes us feel that we are souls akin; for in the theatre an audience will make a positive effort to avoid identifying itself with a figure it recognises as rather ordinary and unromantic.

Johnson is plainly a man we should like but avoid in real life, a pleasant enough fellow but boring to know, and one cannot help a slight feeling of irritation at his response, weak and not unreasonably bewildered, to the challenge that faces him. An audience is a simple and ingenuous entity, and how much more warmly even an intelligent one would have welcomed a figure —with a limp perhaps, a crushed cigarette and a dirty alpaca jacket—who stood up to the third-degree methods of the examiners and awkwardly refused to accept responsibility for anything he had done in the past. This, however, would have defeated the play, the whole purpose of which was "to give an account of a man's life in a new way, taking an ordinary middle-class citizen of our time and then throwing a new light on him and his affairs". There was no question here of refusing to advance on all fronts at once, an inhibition which reduced the characters in *Music at Night* to types recognisable at a glance. It was essential that Johnson should be less than an individual man to make him more of a universal figure. Yet he presents the odd spectacle of a character who is too down to earth but hardly rooted in life at all. We cannot feel emotion for him, only for his situation: ordinary, dull, unperceptive, he stands in the way of the very depth and poignancy which it is the passionate aim of the play to succeed in conveying.

The appeal, therefore, becomes intellectual, and it is in the brilliance of the play's ability to summarise a lifetime, to compress many years into a couple of hours without losing the sense of their length and difficulty, that lie the value and fascination of the piece. Once again the drama of moods and atmospheres gives Priestley his triumph. When his episodes become fantastic, even gruesome, an uncontrolled bogey of melodrama jumps up and begins to leer and dance at the audience, and one feels that Priestley's fancy, which needs to keep very close to life in order to touch magic, has run away from him. But in the naturalistic episodes, when Johnson is seeing crucial moments of his past life re-enacted for him in their true colours, the effect is simple, genuinely pathetic and often moving, because the significance of such scenes is only appreciated when they are set in the larger pattern, in the life as a whole.

Johnson Over Jordan was probably beyond Priestley's powers at the time. The grandeur of the conception cannot be denied, but it was severely mitigated by the crying need for an eloquent vein of poetry that would dispense with some of the deaths-head masks and stagey formalities of dialogue which seemed to critics at the time to be a hangover, too obviously smeared with greasepaint, from the expressionists. Priestley's battle with the critics had already been grumbling for some years, but over this play the fight came out into the open. Even his supporters —James Agate and Ashley Dukes among them—did not care for it, and although they had admired his experiments before, Priestley assumed too readily that they had turned reactionary and were now too much enfeebled by bad plays to hold up the flag of progress and novelty in the theatre. But they were not hostile, merely disappointed—though Agate's particular brand of acid and destructive wit often made it difficult to tell the difference. In 1935 Priestley had written to Agate, "There are some writers who can bide their time and then turn out something like a masterpiece every five years. I am not one of them. I am too restless, too impatient, too prolific of ideas. I am one of the hit-or-miss school of artists." This play, it was felt, must rather sadly be regarded as one of the misses, not because it was searching for something fresh to revive and develop the theatre, but because it failed to find it. *Johnson Over Jordan* was not only unsuccessful in itself but represented a dead end as far as future experiment was concerned; you could go no further down this track.

TO THROW THE WINDOWS OPEN

Music at Night was written against time (in more senses than one) when Priestley returned from America early in 1938, and it was an "attempt to dramatise the mental adventures of a group of people listening to the first performance of a piece of music". This group of people—gossip writer, cabinet minister, hostess, tired lecherous businessman and tired fashionable lady —are brought together in a country house to listen to a new work by a young composer. They are quickly shuffled to their places, for we need very little time to grasp their outward characteristics; later, under the influence of music, they will deepen, and it was Priestley's hope that he would be able to convey the essence of their individual characters in dramatic form by making them behave exactly according to their private thoughts released by the lulling waves of sound.

Attention focusses on them one after the other, and one has the sensation of passing through that blurring of the image which the cinema uses to suggest a switch to memory; and we are now inside the character's mind, watching a scene from life as he wishes it or remembers it, yet retaining the knowledge, from the grouping or the participation of the other characters, that he is inseparably part of a background. Since in our imagination we give to figures of our acquaintance certain character parts to play which are often comically untrue and based on emotional prejudice, Priestley's difficult task was to induce characters, who had been rather speedily established in the audience's mind as true to life, to act at the irresponsible behest of another person's view of them. While the music bores or irritates or softens these people, we are watching their un- bridled fancies playing little tricks to keep them entertained or to keep time and mood with the music. The people expand and blossom in their own imaginings, they cruelly wilt in the projections of the others; and one by one, as the images of memory and desire and speculation flicker past, Priestley cleverly solves the intricate technical problem of giving individuality to stock types by means of total self-revelation.

The second act, like the second movement of the piece, is a gentle adagio very typical of Priestley in mood, bearing the characters back to their moments of regret, the missed opportunity or the happiness that faded before it could be plucked. His temperament comes closest to music in these sad misty atmospheres, and it is an odd guide to his nature that he should always avoid sentimentality in touching such more obviously dangerous casts of feeling, while his attempts to evoke the exuberance of joy and pleasure, as in the last act of *Johnson Over Jordan*, are apt to bring tears of angry embarrassment to the eyes. He is not geared to treat happiness seriously, but only in terms of the comic vision.

The third act contains the matter which it was really his concern to present: "my feeling, steadily hardening into conviction, that we are not really the separate beings we imagine ourselves to be." Despite the vigorous state of dis-harmony in which we live, the clashes between individuals, the bitterness and misunderstanding which we have seen at work poisoning human relations in the first two acts of the play, we are all joined to a higher plane of being which unites us spiritually, holds us together in a free and tranquil society of the soul. Using the same techniques, constantly changing mood and tempo, the third act builds rapidly up to this resolution which is presented when the characters burst one by one into a form of heightened speech, a litany of spontaneous ecstatic realisation that "now there cannot be you or I, or any separate selves, and we are walled in no longer but are free, free!" Once again Priestley is confronted with a language he cannot persuade to leave the ground, words which lack the massive horsepower to soar into celestial poetry, and the effect is therefore more of a dirge than a hymn, more a mutter than a great roar of life.

When Priestley tinkers with universals, tries to find images to carry them, the engine has a habit of sputtering out altogether.

But the point is made, and my own feeling is that the play, tightly constructed and controlled with a fine sense of dramatic timing, is quite strong enough to survive this stumbling rocky patch of writing because the prime interest depends on the fact that these creatures, thrown back on the wayward drifting resources of their minds, are individuals, the very things which the elaborate conclusion sets out to convince us they are not. Priestley has admitted that "the chief weakness of the play is that when I reached the third act I was trying to show that personality, the separate self, is an illusion—a hopeless task in the theatre", and it is a striking example of the way a piece of writing can snatch its skirts away from the clutching embraces of the author and run, almost without his knowledge, in the opposite direction. For the piece is nourished by Priestley's natural sense of the lonely uniqueness of each individual life, and no theory of a vague sublime fellowship has the force to overpower that sense. Personality, according to the instinctive beliefs rooted in the literary character of this author, is plainly no illusion, and the bulk of his work depends on its vagaries for sustenance.

Music at Night is an exciting, thorough-going experiment, consistently followed through to a conclusion that seems to have philosophically resisted what the dramatist longed to do, as though some cosmic power, as airy as one of Priestley's own appeals to dim universals, were determined to keep him tethered to the ground he knew well. But this is a small matter. Among these plays, all technically difficult, all trying to widen the scope of the prose drama and get under the skin of naturalism, all touched with hints and suggestions hard to convey on the stage but worth the effort, only *Johnson Over Jordan* seems to offer Priestley's powers too complex a challenge.

IN ONE PLACE OR ANOTHER

It seemed to me now that Priestley had finally decided after trying most things that the theatre was the place where he would reach his conclusions and obtain his most satisfactory artistic returns. It remained to be seen what he would do after the war. Meanwhile his serious plays did not provide the complete story, indeed, as I had presented them they hardly made a story at all. What of the comedies that during the thirties crept in and out of these more sombre pieces like a jester who insisted on returning at tense and crucial moments? And how had I failed, in pressing only the points that first occurred to me, to remind myself that we were speaking of the theatre, of the blazing and busy curve of Shaftesbury Avenue, of queues for the gallery, shirt-sleeved rehearsals and first-night nerves, and that there was scarcely a month in the thirties when one London playhouse or another did not contain a piece by Priestley?

Slowly, as these years moved towards the explosion of war, the impetus of Priestley's addiction to the theatre increased in speed and quality. It seemed inevitable; he had merely been waiting his moment, showing a rare patience for a writer who normally preferred dash to circumspection. A passionate playgoer in boyhood, with acting ambitions that were confined to the charade, he nevertheless came to the theatre from the undramatic world of letters, from the higher reaches of journalism and retreats into the country to finish a novel, and unlike many others faced with the same wrench, Graham Greene, Charles Morgan and lately Angus Wilson, Priestley seemed at once more at home watching a rehearsal from a lolling stall than staring at the thickening pile of manuscript in an empty room. *The Good Companions*, which he dramatised with Edward Knoblock, set him going at His Majesty's in 1931. Next year came *Dangerous Corner*. Then, to open his long association with J. P. Mitchelhill at the Duchess which quickly matured into joint management, *Laburnum Grove* in 1933 was followed a year later by *Eden End*. Six months later *Cornelius* took audiences (whose "profound intuition", says Priestley, told them there was something wrong with it as a dramatic whole) to glance at life in a city office, and two months after that *Duet in Floodlight*, a brisk light satire on modern publicity methods, opened at the Apollo. *Bees on the Boatdeck*,

a clever attempt to reduce the political scene to terms of
farcical comedy, rich in comic situation and always one of
Priestley's own favourites, was taken to the Lyric in the spring
of 1936, and the very light-weight *Spring Tide* followed at the
Duchess in the summer. In these few years Priestley had un-
furled his banners and displayed them to the best advantage,
and now he was ready to go more seriously into battle.

At the end of 1937 three plays took the stage almost within a
month of each other, and it is characteristic of Priestley's
inability to plot his course carefully through the dangerous
shoals of reputation and career that by the third of them,
People at Sea, he should have risked reversing the critical plaudits
and popular interest he had collected for the other two; for
these were *Time and the Conways* at the Duchess and *I Have Been
Here Before* at the Royalty. *People at Sea* seems cynical, contrived
and unfelt, peopled by bloodless enamelled characters better
suited to a woman's magazine than an intelligent stage, and it
leaves one with the distasteful impression that human experience has been cheapened in order to make the wheel of the
drama come full circle. It seems to me, as it must have seemed
to audiences, an example of Priestley at his worst, dealing with
quite important issues that become trifling and hollow because
their expression is sentimental. But it was followed, a year later
at the St. Martin's, by his most intimate and beautifully timed
domestic comedy, the farcical urban counterpart to *Eden End*
and springing just as thoroughly from the affectionate, touched,
delighted glance over his shoulder to the Yorkshire of his
youth. *When We Are Married*, of all Priestley's plays the least
satisfactory to read because its effects depend on knife-edged
timing and character-playing of the most subtly balanced kind,
is conducted with the tremendous vitality and truth that often
possess an author when he goes back to his roots. The following year, as a fascinating but somewhat unsteady prelude to
the war that burst at the end of it, came *Johnson Over Jordan*,
edging the critics away from Priestley but bringing enthusiasts
for the piece time and again to the New Theatre; and then
Music at Night. At that point it was impossible to predict what

he would do next, and no doubt there were very few indeed who could afford time for such speculation. Priestley, of course, like everyone else, had changed his direction entirely, turning his glance across the perilous waters to where Poland was drawing her eastern bow, and wondering what he could do about it.

VII. A Wartime All-Rounder

THESE IRON DAYS

In the first year of the war, when I was nine, we were living outside Chichester, and it was there one evening, after we had seen the summer sky torn by a dogfight over Tangmere airfield, that I first heard Priestley's voice on the wireless: "a rumbling but resonant voice," he has written, "from which it is difficult to escape." At that time, in the salty electric-blue summer months of 1940, nobody wanted to escape that voice, for it seemed to contain a spirit that the people of this country felt faintly surprised, and rather relieved, that they shared; it was a voice, not this time out of the wilderness, but from a green undisturbable England such as Shakespeare had revealed in Arden and Elgar discovered in his loftiest and calmest melodies. But these glimpses of the golden age, where it was possible to believe we had enjoyed true freedom and a careless fleeting of time, were threatened by an invader; an age of iron could crush them.

Priestley's words, coming over the air on Sunday nights between June and October, set the present struggle intimately into the background of a society and countryside which rooted and nourished us all, uniting a people in a common emotion by painfully sharpening their sense of what they had to lose. Later in the war years, when the wonder and bewilderment had given place to sheer dogged effort, he would be telling them what they must try to gain from all this when the piping times returned; but at that time they were already turning away, becoming individuals once more. This was the moment, and all Priestley's qualities enabled him to rise to it. It is common to compare his effect on the national morale with that of Churchill at the same time. When most people were too astonished to find words, theirs were the only voices.

But we have moved in time too far ahead for Priestley, not far enough for me. He had written one or two books before the war which still needed a word, and only a couple of years ago, in a summer no less remarkable if rather more subdued than those months in 1940, I resolved to spend a few week-ends glancing at them down at Henley. There is no river here, no regatta in July, for this Henley is a small village in Sussex curling up the side of a hill and so shrouded in trees that you cannot see it from the road running between Haslemere and Midhurst, only a few hundred yards away. The beech and pine forests round here, which stand in silences occasionally broken by the buzz of saws and the racket of woodmen living in the village, come close to the houses and overhang their gardens, and further down towards the valley which is wide and deep the sloping meadows begin. There is a pub where we stayed.

As an institution the theatre in this country is something like the actors who work for it; an intense and childlike streak in its nature insists that if you are going to approach it at all, you cannot toy with it in a detached adult way, tossing the occasional play towards a brightly-lit stage in the hope that it will look after itself without any assistance from you. No, the rules of the game require that you should totally involve your time and energies in the theatre, be captured and overwhelmed by it. It would be brash to blame Priestley's failures in the theatre on to the fact that during his two lengthy intimacies with it he never completely locked his study-door and threw away the key, always finding time to regain isolation and turn out a novel or a series of articles, but there is little doubt that his successes were partly due, if these things can be explained at all, to his deep and vital interest in aspects of the theatre other than merely writing for it. He shouldered the burdens of management, he cast plays, arranged salaries, shared late indigestible suppers with actors, he thought and talked theatre from the moment the telephone woke him in the morning. Once he even took the stage, when for several days Frank Pettingell was absent from the cast of *When We are Married* and no actor could be rehearsed in time to replace him. Thus periodically

Priestley has become a man of the theatre entire; it happened first in the middle thirties, and again for a spell after the war. During these periods, particularly the first, that study-door was half open and the dust-sheets occasionally removed to allow the writing of a novel, but a good public-relations man taking you on a tour of Priestley's work would slickly divert your attention from such books. They were written, as it were, when the author's back was turned.

WHEN THE SUN WAS GOING IN

In the winter of 1937 Priestley was staying in Arizona again. He had escaped from the snares and tripwires that entangle a dramatist when he has three plays running simultaneously in London, had watched the New York opening of *Time and the Conways*, and now the cables were shooting to and fro about the American production of *I Have Been Here Before*. In his quiet shack on the ranch he was trying to ease some of the more awkward passages in *Johnson Over Jordan*, and he started a new play called *The Linden Tree* (not, however, the piece subsequently produced under that title). As always, after a moment's rest, he began casting round for new ideas, and into this hurly-burly of plays, theatres, conferences and capital cities there suddenly came a simple straightforward tale, as though it were trying to drag the novelist out of all this noise and uproar and stretch him at ease in the gentler world of fiction. This book, *The Doomsday Men*, took nineteen days to write; it reminds one of a few days' rest snatched by a businessman to avert a nervous breakdown. It is a novel for businessmen too, never for a moment adding to their problems but rather relieving them, fitting neatly inside a folded copy of the *Financial Times* and to be recommended to wives who suffer from brittle social insomnia after giving dinner parties.

The action is romantic, crazy and fast. Lurking at the back of it are three madmen, a millionaire, a scientist and a fanatic, who have built a remote fantastic folly of a castle in the depths of the Arizona desert from which they intend to destroy the world. There is a girl with them, as soft and lovely to the imagination as a ravished princess, and there are young men determined to rescue her. If the story contains quite familiar ingredients, the speed and vitality of the telling contrive to transfigure them; the people have bright original faces, and coming events never too obviously cast their shadows before. I read the book in an afternoon and more than once—and this happens rarely in Priestley's work—I was carried away not simply by the natural energy of his prose but by the beauty of it. Passages of description in the later part of the novel, when he was plainly in spate and moved to normally unattainable heights by the spontaneous act of creation, touched the mind with such a sharp electricity of image that I had to put the book down for a moment and breathe again; Priestley des- cribes them as "one or two pretty little bits of writing", and I suppose he is right. From the point of view of construction, this was probably the best novel Priestley had so far written, except *Benighted*, and they are both thrillers of a kind; in the first Priestley was making the attempt to reconcile the plotty novels of crime and detection which he flipped through in bed with fiction of more serious purpose, and in the second he was merely writing a novel to flip through in bed and to keep himself occupied "in a happy if brittle dream" for close on three weeks when his mood was restless.

The *Doomsday Men* was published in 1938 and early the following year the B.B.C. asked Priestley to write a novel suitable for serialisation on the air. The result was a catchphrase which echoed above the crash of bombs during the first years of the war and a book which can be reasonably judged only if we place it in the context of the time, the medium and the purpose. *Let the People Sing* emerges now as a gay, heartening, pathetic and somewhat embarrassing romance of the concert troupe in conflict with big business and die-hard toryism, a little free world against the black monster of fascism. Had it never been written Priestley's subsequent reputation might have benefited considerably, but many people who needed such vigorous comfort as this book provided in the fearful months at the close of 1939 would have been much the poorer. There never was a Jolly Jack: this affirmation, which Priestley made recently in *Thoughts in the Wilderness*, may have surprised the legend, but it failed to dispel it. Jolly Jack is an easy news-story nickname to catch the eye and it has worked wonders of misleading for years. *Let the People Sing*, which seems now to have snatched the genuine comic spirit from *The Good Companions* and battered every ounce of honest fun from it, must have succeeded in carrying Priestley's name for jollity across the war and establishing it, quite unfairly, on the other side when he was giving us such pieces as *The Linden Tree* and *Bright Day*, more heart-breaking than hearty, closer to real tears than false laughter. It is superficial, it is saddening. *Let the People Sing*, despite many amusing and effective touches, must be dismissed to be fair to it, for it was written on the surge of a particularly stormy wave and when it was no longer needed sank back into the sea. It remains one of the few books by Priestley that I would recommend no one to read. The aisles in which people were intended to roll were removed at much the same time as the unexploded bombs in the London streets.

The first instalment of *Let the People Sing* was broadcast on the day war was declared. Earlier the sirens had wailed, people hurried into shelters with their hearts pounding, and nothing had happened. And then the months passed, and still nothing happened: not here at least; but in Europe the winter mutterings of armoured Germany brought the tension nearer, and as that marvellous spring thickened into summer, it was thought possible from the downs above Folkestone to catch the glint of sunlight on alien steel helmets across the Channel. Churchill had spoken: the national fist was clenched. But the mood of the country still flickered with doubts, perplexities and a humorous denial of both, a wonder that this should have happened at all and the curious and heady excitement of challenge, an uprooted mixture of feelings that Priestley felt and saw and understood with a deep urgency that gave him the power to speak for it. No judgment was required to divine what the people wanted—he had never been much of a hand at calculating his appeal—since he was finding words for precisely what he wanted himself. Unless you were cramped by a false adolescent sophistication, the pretended cynicism into which young men often retreat when faced with the mild horror of patriotism, it was impossible not to be moved by the exquisitely and candidly proud portrait of a country poised with a kind of fatuous sang-froid on the brink of destruction.

The *Postscripts* began on 5th June, just after Dunkirk, and they came to an end on the 20th October when the Luftwaffe had already launched its first blitz on London. During those months, from studios here and there all over the capital, Priestley quite unconsciously encountered those moments of greatness which, rare in the lives of any but the greatest writers, suddenly vindicate as well as clarify the efforts of a lifetime in the use of words. One of his memories of the early autumn of 1940, recounted in *Delight*, is of getting out of London after an exhausting sleepless week of broadcasting and writing articles and finding himself, with gin and tonic and potato crisps, alone in the bar parlour of a village pub in Oxfordshire on Friday evening, feeling "only an unfathomable sense of peace and quiet and remoteness". That sweet hour might also have held fulfilment for him, for after twenty years of striving to display the conflicting weathers of individual life, to celebrate the magic of the world he lived in, to discover what influences and powers lay at the back of the human scene, to forge a style which offered his findings in the simplest terms, he had been able, in speaking solely and naturally of himself, to strike a host of common moments at a very uncommon time. Not for nothing had the public figure delivered his grim advice from platforms all over the world; the playwright, seeking the dramatic device that caught a situation perfectly, had not written in vain; the novelist, who always saw the movement and the pattern as well as perceiving the exaggerated detail that conveyed the truth, came forward well qualified for this new, difficult and important task.

I never thought, and I do not think now, that it is possible to overrate the effect of these broadcasts at a crucial hour in history. As to their literary value, if one can speak of it in the same breath, they read now as evocatively as they were heard at the time; they re-create the tensions that were felt, and then at once relax them. It is odd that one should not even require to place them in historical context to return to the pleasure, and almost to the relief, of hearing them, for they make the context as they go along, and that is probably due to the fact that Priestley introduced much that seemed irrelevant to the immediate concern of war, always giving it a twist that brought it close to his theme. That large steaming meat-and-potato pie in the Bradford shop-window, the visit to Margate that captured the sweating promenades of pre-war summers, the references to Thomas Hardy and Dickens that brought them alive again in a crisis that might have killed them for ever, "the round green hills dissolving into the hazy blue of the sky": Priestley set these points of reference in people's minds as a valuable background to the fight that needed to be won, and they are touched with such an acute sense of their immeasurable value, so serious and honest and urgent a feeling, that they have not faded away into a few sentimental images that once worked a miracle. *Postscripts* was the first really effective barrage in the war Priestley was fighting; this time, rather different from the past, no one needed persuading, for it happened to be everyone else's war as well.

Now Priestley's duty was plain: to observe aspects of the war and present them "in their simplest, but profoundest, terms", not only to speak to this country, but also for it, to contribute to this present battle as much by preparing a hopeful and constructive path into the confused serenities of the post-war world as by discovering realistic ways of heartening what had now become an enormous and favourable audience. He continued to convey this country's cornered snarling across the ocean in broadcasts to America; in 1941 he wrote a book, *Out of the People*, which presented the arguments for and against democracy, that muddled concept which had just been so severely put to the test. In the following year there was an illustrated book about the strength behind the war effort, and later he wrote a factual account of the part women were playing in making arms, working in canteens and joining the services. And in 1942 he published the first of the three novels that drew on the war for their subject: this was *Blackout in Gretley*, followed in 1943 by *Daylight on Saturday* and two years later, when we had reached the verge of peace, by *Three Men in New Suits*.

TO MEET THE CHALLENGE

Chichester, where I had heard one of those postscripts, was twelve miles from the village of Henley and sometimes I took the bus over the subtle remote ranges of the South Downs and went to the cinema there or looked at the cathedral where I had once heard the drone of bombers. I remembered the atmospheres; I had seen German fighters zoom low and litter the dog-rose lanes with cartridge-cases. But then, at the end of 1940, we had moved away from that grey and pleasant front-line city to a small town in Hampshire where for four years the war was confined to a few jettisoned incendiaries breaking like a litter of bright fairy campfires on a hillside behind the house, and I had no sense of an atmosphere other than childhood. Perhaps this absence of any sense of violent war during those years gave me a slight feeling of fatigue when I was trying to discover at Henley what Priestley had written at that time, whether it could still make an impact. Usually one can anticipate that only books written under the compulsion of vivid and sensitive memory about so disturbing an experience as war are likely to find a permanent place in literature, for the perspective of the actual time is always quick to dissolve and anything written then assumes the nature of an interim report. Although I own a slight prejudice against the historical novel, I am sure that the issues of particular wars as well as their atmospheres are best conveyed by an imaginative novelist writing from the heights of the future.

This long introduction suggests that one is about to praise Priestley's war novels by excusing them, and the suggestion is probably true. They were written with a purpose: a gift for narrative is a small cog in the war machine but a valuable one and, after stirring by his broadcasts a large number of people to clamour for his books, he gave them what he thought would keep them sufficiently entertained to deflect minds from the struggle and would also hearten them by showing one or two of the ways in which the struggle was being conducted. *Blackout in Gretley*, superficially a straightforward and moderately absorbing detective novel, attempts to expose the dangers of fifth-column and talking too freely in public, the complex system established to track down and defeat enemy espionage, the wartime attitudes that are foolish or dangerous to strike, and the variety of new values and conditions to which people had to become accustomed. Priestley has a gift for making bad times brighter by showing them much darker than they are, while he manages to retain a vigorous actuality in his descriptions. The gritty rain that seems to drive incessantly through the pages of *Blackout in Gretley*, the drab pubs where you can only get beer, the aching Midland streets, not only served this purpose; they also suggested the dark evil forces of war that were dancing in the world as triumphantly as rain on a tin roof—"a great and ever-widening black pit into which men, women, houses, whole cities, went slithering". The book was a protest buried deep in a racy, conventional and at times somewhat unconvincing thriller, and it was "a story of—and for—wartime". No more is claimed for it. The sales were enormous, partly because the appetite for reading matter was at its sharpest in this dark period of the war. It is more than possible that many younger people came to Priestley for the first time in *Blackout in Gretley*, since paper restrictions had kept his pre-war books out of print ever since *Postscripts* created a demand for his work.

The hints of an attitude to war which appeared in this novel are expanded creatively in the pages of its more serious successor, *Daylight on Saturday*. Priestley had now had time to observe more widely the effect of brusque and often cruel change on the people of a country at war, and he had deepened into an awareness of the innumerable small and hopeless

tragedies that lay littered along its margins. He set out to write
a novel which could intensely catch the noisy artificial atmosphere in which people were forced to conduct lives of a very
stark reality. To achieve this, he chose to set his story, if such it
can be called, entirely within the workrooms, canteens and
machine-shops of an aircraft factory, never taking his readers
outside its doors except in the furtive glimpses of people whose
minds were not on the job. One by one the characters are
introduced, neatly but never harshly analysed, then pushed
back to take their places in the pattern of daily life in a factory.
For this is less a novel than a pattern of events from which
moods and personalities are allowed to emerge; we do not
move upwards to a climax but merely across the work-room
floor, through to the offices, along to the boardroom, picking
up the different stories and relationships as we go. The atmosphere is supplied by the hard remorseless light under which the
eleven-hour shifts pursue their tasks, while the hammering of
machines infects the prose with a hard and virile clarity.

The noise, the rhythm, the changeless routine, the gleam of
metal and the fierce light, these are the signature of war, the
mark of evil scrawled across so many tired sunken faces, and
the way Priestley conveys these realities and keeps them
grinding and glittering in the background of his book is a
sudden return to the near-poetry that stretched itself to the
length of essays in his earlier novels. Here, however, the writing
is not only powerful but integrated, essential to the piece; we
are in the presence of a prose that is spare, tense, purposeful.
Here the protest against war may have come to Priestley in the
more hysterical form of a creative rather than an intellectual
impulse, but that only ensures that he keeps it more firmly in
control. It also encourages in him a livelier interest in the
characters and a deeper sympathy for them: they are people,
and also, something unusual in Priestley, studies in character.
The works superintendent has a wife who went mad during
an awkward childbirth, and he is haunted by the pain of
it and the crude need for women; Miss Shipton, the welfare
officer, is dragging out an anxious love-affair with a married

schoolmaster living miles away; Bolton who was destroyed in all but his bitter anger when a stray bomb killed his wife and family: these are unusual characters for Priestley, and they are shown with a delicacy of feeling that is a counterpart of his passionate hatred of war. Both spring from a deep concern.

This concern also turned to the future and *Three Men in New Suits* is the rather slapdash story of three soldiers who return from the army in hope and find a world that is awkwardly changed and reluctant to take them back. The wife of one has been unfaithful; another finds that he fits clumsily into the family again; the third rushes into a jazzy job and the wrong woman's arms. However, by coming together again into the old comradeship, they manage to avert disaster and revive hope; they must build the future, not be crushed by someone else trying to build it for them. Throughout the war Priestley had been anxious lest, as soon as peace came, the lesson should be ignored, and we would merely drift back into a lazy approximation to the old unequal world. A violent and destructive outburst, like a war or a revolution, reduces the old world to a heap of rubble but it does not necessarily lay foundations as well; an ideal in conflict with a reality is apt to be defeated as soon as the reality is destroyed. This is what happened. The Labour government of 1945 was the practical answer to the cries Priestley raised in this book.

Since then, in his disappointment, Priestley had made the inevitable political retreat to what is vaguely termed humanism and usually means a wise and carefully considered one-man policy that is capable, in the face of an international scene constantly on the change, of frequent contradictions and inconsistencies but no change of heart. A writer is never forgiven for teaching lessons in a work of fiction unless he can unavoidably make dramatic issues out of them, and Priestley, still preoccupied with his task of forcing people to face the future intelligently, took no trouble to soften his blows in *Three Men in New Suits*, thereby softening them in quite the wrong way. One or two passable characters lounge through the book (Uncle Rodney deserves richer pages than these) but they are disguises for viewpoints, and we are even wary of scenes that would have been touching in another context. But no more of this: as far as Priestley was concerned, the book had served its turn as soon as Labour moved across the House of Commons. It seemed a pity that after so many explosions their powder was no longer dry.

COME OUT INTO THE SUNLIGHT

Priestley had written five plays during the war. In 1942 *Goodnight, Children* was withdrawn after a short run at the New Theatre, probably failing because it mocked an institution—radio—which Priestley himself had often praised as contributing magnificently to the war effort. I tried to read it but, despite some light sardonic scenes worthy of his best comedy, it seemed a little heavy-handed. Possibly, since the B.B.C. became rather more self-aware and jokes at its expense a commonplace of daily journalism and the comic turn, the funny-bone has been tickled for too long on this score and now feels nothing. Priestley did, however, make sharper use of much the same material twelve years later in *Low Notes on a High Level*.

Two other plays, both produced in London in 1944, were never intended to be effective beyond the special purpose for which they were written. *Desert Highway* was a gift to the Army Bureau of Current Affairs for one-night stands in army camps, while *How are They at Home?* was a light topical play designed to be taken by E.N.S.A. to men serving overseas. The former attempts an interesting experiment. In two acts Priestley tells the story of a crew whose tank has broken down near an old highway in the Syrian desert and the way in which they all slowly realise that they may have reached the moment of death; and between the two acts he interposes a scene that jumps back twenty centuries to a similar situation in the vague biblical mists of near-eastern history, using the same characters and showing how the tensions and concerns of human life have scarcely changed in all that time.

This device, if it deepens the implications of the second act when possible death is drawing nearer, is somewhat unsatisfactory for the superficial reason that the contemporary soldiers are so sharply etched in the first act that we wish to continue hearing about them without interruption. But if we can quell this prejudice, it proves to be an effective way of suggesting the immensity of time which stretches with an even more arid cruelty than the desert itself and the dilemma of the individual human life dropped down on to the sands of history for a spell and searching there for hope and belief. The almost Christian comfort which Priestley untypically dispenses must have made an impression on audiences in time of war, even if we feel now that it shows those woolly aspirations to realms of poetic expression which so often confound his lyrical or idealistic moments in the plays; it is almost as though we were listening to the effusions of a country rector who believes he runs a close second to his admired Tennyson.

A year earlier than this, however, a play called *They Came to a City* had opened its career at Bradford and then moved to enjoy a long run at the Globe Theatre, and this play is unquestionably Priestley's most successful attempt to contrive a drama in which the quite obvious element of debate was not resented by audiences. For once the frank idealism is totally disarming. The set is bright with sunlight, turning to a sky of intense blue and then purple as the evening comes; the action takes place outside the walls of "a strange city", never described except in terms of the moods it evokes in the characters, the vague idea of it romantically handed to the imaginations of the audience. The nine people, who represent a fair cross-section of English society, have no notion of what curious power brought them to this place: was it death, or a dream? One remembers a geyser exploding, another feels he must have been knocked out by a golf-ball, a third recalls going through a tunnel on a train to Tewkesbury. But their interest in the reason for being there soon melts under the warmth of their speculations about the city below the walls; and at dawn the gate slowly opens, they enter.

The second acts shows them emerging from the city at dusk,

having spent the day in the sincere, moral, friendly and profoundly happy climate of its community life. Some it does not suit—the slick small-time financier, the landed gentleman with his muffled inarticulate pride in the old order, the bank-clerk's selfish wife who cannot bear to see her husband want something else so much—and these people stupidly and rather tragically trail back to the disordered world from which they came. The charwoman and a well-bred daughter seeking release from her mother's tedious routine of watering-place retirement are both determined to go back and throw their lives into the happiness and wonder of the city. But for the two who fell in love that morning—the stoker and the waitress who want this city so deeply—there is a conflict which produces one of the most gripping moments of dramatic tension in all Priestley's plays. She needs the city with all her heart; but he, an idealist, a rebellious rough-and-ready thinker, knows that he must return to the old world to spread the good news, to make sure people discover that such a city as this exists. And as they move away, to the echo of a passionate ideological eloquence that is saved by its sincerity from casting the audience into embarrassment, Priestley has succeeded at the last moment in conveying his belief that the new Utopian world of co-operation, energy and truth is still within our reach. For the ideal has been neither stated nor implied; it has been presented in human terms.

The technical problem of giving the city a sufficiently vigorous identity to attract an audience, to strike a chord so inspiring that cynicism fleets away, has been satisfactorily solved in theory, though I was never quite happy about it. The notable characteristic of most Utopias is that we do not want to visit them; we are fond of our drab, discoloured old world. But Priestley has all the answers. If we cannot accept the city, that is because we are not ready for it, our imaginations are not working creatively but in a set pattern. It is preferable to have a picture of the place so misty that our objections are negative rather than so detailed that we positively cannot stand the thought of it. If the characters had remained the stock figures they at first appeared to be, no audience could have accepted the healthy-minded jamboree that seemed to be going on behind that wall. But fortunately we glimpse the light of the city in their eyes when they return, and we trust it: they have plainly been moved, delighted and renewed—no less than many audiences in the darkest centre of the war when green shoots of hope were beginning to enliven a winter landscape.

THE MUSIC OF OUR EXPERIENCE

At Henley, as the week-ends moved past, we were still some way from winter, but during the weeks in London, cycling down the Bayswater Road towards the office, I often caught a hurried glimpse of that smoky autumnal gold which Priestley captures so magically in *Bright Day*. We were, I suppose, just past the middle of September and one could still read in the open air. It was hard to imagine, sitting there on delicate afternoons, that a book like *Bright Day* should ever need to be written, for it is at first sight a protest against the present. But because the book is emotional, the most deeply and disturbingly so of all Priestley's works, it is also an enthusiastic shout in favour of the present, and the logical integration of these two opposing emotional views of our post-war time provides the tension which runs beneath the development of the story. From the first sentence there is no doubt that we are in for a serious novel, and it very soon becomes clear that *Bright Day* is so naturally conceived, and the details given are so unconsciously the correct and essential ones, that Priestley has at last been carried away by a sudden explosion of his total experience, both of writing and of life. All his previous work has tended towards this moment; all his years of living come forward to serve the present purpose.

It is the only novel (apart from the less serious *Blackout in Gretley*) Priestley has chosen to write in the first person, and this in itself was a risk. The owner of a public personality can never conceal it very successfully behind a fictional incognito,

for readers begin an idle game of picking out traits they recognise
and then smugly feel they have somehow caught him out. A
first-person hero also limits the range of a novel, and up to this
time Priestley had always compensated in scope for what he
lacked in depth. The first of these dangers he countered by
putting as much of himself into the central figure as a book by
no means purely autobiographical would allow, and slowly,
by making the pipe-smoking middle-aged Gregory Dawson
seem more than a little Priestleyan, he achieves a character
who is a projection of himself managed in a detached, ironic
and disarming way. The book is written as though Dawson had
met Priestley and liked him, finding that they had certain
attitudes in common but quickly discovering that certain
aspects of his temperament needed to be watched. Priestley and
his hero are too close to be parted, but they are not the same
man.

I found this worth a moment of emphasis, for it is interesting
in his most subjective novel that Priestley should have retained
his objectivity for the writing. A sour dyspeptic script-writer
tired to death of films and lonely as hell looks back into the
glowing past to catch a glimpse of a magic family he knew,
days on the moors, the tragic break-up of an untroubled age:
that is one way of looking at the story, and on the face of it it
seems almost doomed to be received with negative sentimental
tears in back-parlours where novels of nostalgia are achingly
consumed. But the emotion conveyed is positive; it is tense and
real; and it is made so because Priestley has discovered the
highest form of detachment of which a writer is capable: he
has not come forward to convey himself, but is standing back
to create himself. The result is an affectionate but not uncritical
picture of everything this world has made him feel, a testament
that insists on its demand to be taken seriously, an emotional
statement that summarises the world of our time beneath a
story which without effort bestrides three generations of men.

Compared with *Bright Day*, all Priestley's previous excursions
into the novel may be regarded as somewhat disorderly
treasure chests, or lucky dips, in which there was something for

every reader; or, to put it less crudely, they were not so much
rounded stories established within a single mood and driving to
a strict purpose, but broadly designed collections of set-pieces,
essays in experience linked by narrative. Thus one can always
select from the novels certain passages, like Mr. Smeeth's visit
to the Queen's Hall in *Angel Pavement* or the public meeting in
Festival at Farbridge, which rise above the general level of the
book and succeed in describing their particular occasions or
experiences better than they have ever been described elsewhere. They are made, it seems, for anthologies. But *Bright Day*
might never have been written if the problems of construction,
the untrammelled movement in time of which a man's mind is
capable at certain turning-points in his life, had not been so
difficult to solve. Once again the book's excellence probably
springs from the laziness of the author; he needs something
technically big, apparently impossible, to stir him to action.
Unquenchable energy in itself does not produce disciplined
writing, as the example of Dickens so clearly shows; it requires
the challenge either of intractable material or of difficult
technique.

Dawson, isolated at an hotel in Cornwall working at breakneck speed on a dim script, has reached that sour moment of
decision in his forties when it will soon be too late for him to
strike out in another direction; he is tired, disillusioned and
frightened. A chance encounter takes him back to the Bruddersford of his youth before the first war, and while the surface of his
mind is occupied with the script and the drab hotel days, the
darker and almost forgotten places in his thoughts are free to
reach back in time and piece together that world which at first
seemed so lost and improbable. Slowly, with all the excitement
of a creative act, as though it were a new experience, the years
to which he had never given a thought take shape, glow in their
recollected colours and join hands with the present. There is no
sense of escapism, of unnaturally gilding the past, in Dawson's
effort of memory; unconsciously he is engaged in conquering
time, in drawing the strands of his personality together, so that
the integration of past and present will include the future too

and make it no problem. A man's life totally exists in a single
moment: Alan was saying it in *Time and the Conways*, and of all
the time theories, however cleverly we disprove it with an
application of logic, this approaches most closely to the
emotional truth, the truth we want to believe because it
helps us.

In Bruddersford the boy Dawson, travelling home from the
wool office where he worked, was enchanted by a bright
nonsensical family chattering and laughing on the top of the
tram: three girls, one brusque and green-eyed, another hazy
and angelic, the third calm and appraising, and a young man
fierce with energy and humour. He watches them across the
magic distance of loneliness, then finds to his delight that they
are the family of his employer, the gentle and smiling Mr.
Alington. Parties, picnics, evenings of music, sudden odd
encounters with one or other of them, begin to fill his life;
curious vague people, who existed on the fringes of this circle,
just out of the light, come forward, vanish, reappear, as though
they were characters created by memory, not caught for a
moment in its wandering speculative glance. For remembering
is the most perfect act of creation; experience is never real,
though it may be pleasurable or painful, until we discover it in
ourselves in the light of what happened subsequently. This,
in the Alingtons and their circle, was tragedy; despite the
unbelievable summers that never moved, the autumns that
lingered and brought rain, a moment arrived on a June day
in 1914 when one of the girls fell to her death, and from that
point the thunder could always be heard at the back of the sky.
The war came, and Dawson left Bruddersford. Only once or
twice in the twenties did some chance meeting put him in
touch with the unhappy days that had followed for the Alingtons. He was soon involved in films, hurrying between Hollywood and London, fighting for his life in a world not worth
fighting for, until he was eventually tossed up at an hotel in
Cornwall to complete a script against time. And then it all
began again.

Towards the end of *Midnight on the Desert* Priestley recalls meeting William Gerhardi very late one night and "listening to his theory that true art is a fourth dimensional account of things". To judge experience and to see the strange beauty of it, the pattern, one must free the mind from the domination of time. With Proust, "the recaptured experience seemed to exist magnificently for its own sake. . . . It was as if now that Time had stopped roaring on our ears, we could listen to the music of our experience." After years of contemplating the problem, of plunging into the dream of time and trying to find a place there from which its distorted shapes and misleading mirrors could be placed in some form of artistic perspective, Priestley found the answer in *Bright Day*; improbably enough, in a novel. Always his inclination drew him to the theatre and until 1946 his best level of performance was doubtless to be found there. But a play, as both *Time and the Conways* and *I Have Been Here Before* must have proved to him, would not take this; it was too tight, too fast and unreflective a medium. The intensity of the drama needed to be combined with the range of a novel, but this time the breadth of vision encompassed time, not space, the individual inner pattern rather than the collective social picture. Almost every new turn that Priestley's career has taken has also extended the range of his gifts; every departure adds to, instead of confirms, the string of letters after his name. *Bright Day*, however, was the revolutionary change, and it only happened once. Priestley, as well as Gregory Dawson, realised at the end of the war that his mind was involuntarily turning a full circle around him from a particular and very decisive moment he had reached in experience.

The shuttling back and forth between one time and another is contrived with a technical mastery so unobtrusive that the reader is hardly aware that the changes exist. The narrative is fluent, and the devices for catching time on the hop never depend on coincidence or a jolt of the unexpected. During every moment of the book, however absorbing a scene's particular detail or mood, Priestley makes us conscious that we are dealing in that moment, not just with an incident, but with the whole of a man's life. Each second hangs in the balance created by the mind's total detachment from time, and its weight and influence are exactly recorded. As to both thought and language, *Bright Day* is Priestley's most precise piece of work, a stern refusal to compromise with any of the demands it made on his powers.

Wise, moving and optimistic, the book must be regarded as his deepest and most mature contribution to the experimental science of living. Even if we wince slightly at the somewhat high-flown fanfare of hope that is sounded at the end, this does not prevent us feeling that a step forward has been taken: not in the art of fiction perhaps, although the scheme of the book represents one of the many minor originalities to be found in Priestley's work, but in illustration of the way that in a man's life reference to the past can cure the present and provide the future with energy, simply because only the present can give a lucid and dispassionate view of the past. That is why the book is unsentimental and rich in imaginative substance (the substance of his previous novels had been supplied more by invention than imagination), and why it is ludicrous to mention escapism when talking of Priestley. No one could be less frequently victimised by a longing to return to his boyhood; he is merely aware that his roots are still there and that the tree is still growing.

For Priestley the war was over now, and so was my summer of week-ends at Henley. Now the country had turned the corner into autumn, to face winds that had a gusty northern edge, to find the leaves swirling and settling. Walking up the lane or watching the spread of valley, one could almost feel that this was the landscape, the wide hazy moorland tinged with heather, which Gregory Dawson had evoked in memory: it might not look the same in detail, but it carried a similar atmosphere. Some books that we read chime so subtly with us that their echo becomes permanent, the lesser among them coinciding with merely a mood or a stage of development so that they are always remembered and re-read years later probably with disappointment, but the greater revisited again and again, not necessarily because they are good books but because they have become ours.

For me *Bright Day* is such a book as this, its spirit as haunting and lucid as a memory of my own life, and I could talk of the people, hardly aware that I was inventing recollections never written by Priestley. In a curious way this novel strikes behind specific memories and throws a little light on the memory that we all might be said to share in common, the sense of race, our roots in history; it is only a chink in the curtain perhaps, but it has the effect of making one feel more human, more mortal yet more sharply alive. This is the condition of mind which the sight of hills or the sound of music inspires, a climate in which beliefs take root and one's convictions harden, growing a shade wiser.

SHOWING THE CROWD A VISION

From the deep optimism generally felt at the end of the war, the years passed into the more superficial and somewhat manufactured optimism that organised, in the growing threat of world disintegration, the constructive Festival of Britain in 1951. This poised, elaborate and influential celebration ran during the summer of that year, but for months previously its gaiety, so brittle that it sometimes seemed made entirely of plastic like so many of the exhibits, had dominated the newspapers and genuinely infected the country with a little much-needed pride in itself. Priestley's contribution to the Festival was his longest novel, *Festival at Farbridge*, written at top speed during 1950 and published in the following August.

The book was a relative failure (though not in America where it received a generous press) and one of the reasons for this was probably the fatigue that set in almost before the Festival itself had got under way; we wanted no more of it, our greedy appetite for acid colours, modern shapes, bright new departures, had been satiated, and we needed grey skies and softer voices back again to recover from the profusion of novelty. Apart from this, which is hardly a sufficient explanation, we feel slightly distrustful of a work of fiction which is tied to a particular contemporary event, as though this disqualified its

bona fides, made it automatically guilty of rolling logs or grinding axes, and brought it almost insolently close to us. With a
part of our mind we like to believe that we are in a timeless
uncommitted world when we are reading a novel, even if the
author's aim is to illuminate an aspect of living in our own age.
For references to Sir Robert Boothby or the Security Council
we have our newspapers delivered every day; if they crop up
in the pages of a novel, however, we are conscious of a faint
disgust which suggests that we want a writer to behave as a
divine superior being, writing of human affairs in situations we
recognise, but never pinning down an actual month or real
person to bring the forces of unreality flushing into the dream.

The title alone of *Festival at Farbridge* seemed to me a psycho-
logical error: Farbridge sounds dull, small and almost too
fictional, and Festival sounds, not to put too fine a point on it,
jolly. A feeling arose when the book was published that this
was just the sort of novel Priestley *would* decide to write. During
the past decade his politics, like those of Cleeton in *Daylight on
Saturday*, had succeeded in offending everybody; authors, he
had proved, should never interfere with the serious and responsible business of statecraft. All nations, however triumphant,
feel a certain guilt and distaste when they have tasted peace
after a bitter war, and they are apt to make an inward denial of
those who have spoken or acted for them during the struggle,
even as they publicly celebrate their names. A man never
recovers from a great moment; one should die at Trafalgar.

For all that, *Festival at Farbridge* contains the most consistently
comic invention in the whole of Priestley's work, including
The Good Companions. This comedy is more resourceful than
profound, more a product of high spirits than vision, but the
design of the book is so concentrated and closely woven that,
once it begins to move heavily forward, the touch-and-run
helter-skelter of comic situation produces a satisfactory humorous effect of its own. A character previously introduced appears
at the right moment to perform the right but unpredictable
function; an explosive surprise is always lying in wait. In
Midnight on the Desert Priestley wrote that his novels "may not

seem—in fact, I know by this time that they certainly do not seem—closely-knit, severely logical in their action, yet that is how they appear to me." That was in 1937, when he spoke the truth; now, however, he has added both *Bright Day* and *Festival at Farbridge*, the first a narrative spare and intense in its flow, the second a neat, economical and complex pattern in which he has organised diverse material with a strict hand. One of the reasons for this, perhaps, is that the book never caught fire in his imagination, and he therefore never dashed exuberantly beyond the invention prompted by the book's original plan. On the other hand, there are unmistakable signs that certain elements, in theory essential to the plan, never came properly alive at all and had to be constantly injected to keep the blood flowing, while others took over from Priestley to the extent of giving us the impression that they are dictating too fast for his shorthand.

Three central characters dominate the action, and they are introduced in the same fashion as the three similar figures in *The Good Companions*, by means of long chapters describing the events which led to their meeting. Laura is a young secretary, independent of mind, tart but rather romantic; Theodore Jenks is an unnaturally large bronze-haired young man with a diffidence that sometimes irks even the reader, let alone Laura; but the hero of the piece is the bulky, proud, effervescent and knavish Commodore Tribe with his eyes "as busy and wicked as mice". The three of them chance to share a table in a dainty Farbridge café one rainy morning, they are all at loose ends and wonder if anything can be done to join them into a knot. The challenge of a drab wet town to be conquered and provided with sunshine fires the Commodore to suggest that they set about changing the public mind as far as a local festival is concerned. Making capital out of municipal politics, using every weapon that comes to hand, fighting institutions, court-ing individuals, shouting or charming or just keeping quiet, they succeed in their aim and the town breaks into unac-customed fireworks.

According to the tradition of the comic epic, a reverse always comes hot on the heels of a triumph, moments of despair are suddenly brightened, and tension is created by the very speed at which the activities are conducted; like a holiday camp, it never lets up for a moment. On the other hand, these are not organised games in the sense that we are lashed into a frenzy of spurious delight at the author's crafty bidding. Priestley has still avoided becoming the sly cynical entertainer who puts his tongue in his cheek while he serves up a helping of just what his readers want. You may not enjoy what is called rumbustious humour, but its expression is just as close and natural to Priestley as the more sophisticated wit that gleams in his essays or the slight grin he hardly even shares with his readers behind the serious front of his polemical writings. He is not a man of many masks which can be whipped on and off at will, defying the critic to discover a real Priestley behind them; he is a writer of several faces, a hydra of letters, all of which are seen to be part of the same creature. As soon as you dismiss one of these faces as foolish or insignificant, not your type of writer at all, another springs up in its place. He is versatile in mood, in concern, in technique and in the art of writing itself.

Theodore Jenks hails from the colonies and is visiting England for the first time. This gave Priestley a chance of having a dispassionate observer at his disposal, someone in a position to view this country freshly as a place that was curious, foreign, eccentric. Unhappily the disadvantage of the unprejudiced eye is that it soon becomes fixed in the dull glazed expression of a person taking too much in and giving too little in return, and this is the trouble with Theodore. Laura is little better. Again Priestley loses her in the crowd and seems only to drag her out against his artistic will, to keep the pattern formal. Sexual love has never played much part in his work; no one brought up in the hearty prosperous chapel of the nonconformist middle class before 1914 can write about that subject with anything but a childlike and ingenuous romanticism, as though he were still gazing from afar at one of the girls in the choir. Priestley never moves beyond the magic of first encounters, the gentle touches of feeling when the heart is beginning to open to another person, the melancholies of parting, misunderstanding, unrequited love. Between Rose and Edward in *They Walk in the City*, between Inigo and Susie in *The Good Companions*, these innocent affairs had been tenderly described; they belonged to a world where the distant glimpse of love, the mind charged with fantasies, was the usual condition of mind for young men and women, when moments of blissful union were so rare as to be a source of wonder and astonishment. H. G. Wells was a master of these touching awkward moments in youthful lives, and Priestley, born into the same society, naturally followed him. But Laura and Theodore are the more sophisticated children of another age, and Priestley would have stumbled over a slight embarrassment if he had been required to describe the closer, more direct and less stuttering relationship that might suit them more naturally. Thus he keeps them moving only with an effort, to make them play their parts in the unfolding of the story; inside, as people, they are both inert, uncreated.

But Commodore Tribe, that bluff and plausible rogue, stirs the scene to life as soon as he enters; it is he who seems to snap his fingers and bring the other characters scuttling forward, he who holds Priestley's interest and keeps his hand firm and confident from first moment to last. The book owes everything to this high-handed, overbearing poseur with his charming and specious and childlike ways. He is the electricity in the atmosphere, the moment we wait for, the time to sit up in our seats. In writing *Festival at Farbridge* Priestley could no longer rely on vitality to extend to every corner of the enormous world he had chosen to display; this was work for a young man and he was now in his middle fifties. He therefore required something other than his own creative vigour to carry the book away, to keep the new faces popping up, and this work was performed by the Commodore. Minor characters are either created individually and with a great expenditure of energy, thereafter running away with their author as they do in Dickens, or they are by-products of the vitality that has been poured into the hero and they become exactly the kind of people he would meet. This represents one of the differences between this later comedy and *The Good Companions*.

There is another, more important. *Festival at Farbridge* is a broad social picture, compressed within an action lasting only a few weeks, of an England for which Priestley does not care as much as he did. Nothing has blunted the accuracy of his observation, but his heart has been submerged and that former glow, which cast an almost imperceptible mood of melancholy that seems inseparable from the comic vision, has drained away like the setting sun, leaving the background drab and grey. For this reason the book is never moving. The geniality is there, the warmly amused sympathy for the way people are, but the humour comes entirely from situations, crises, débâcles, triumphs, the manner in which individual scenes are presented rather than the way in which they are seen. I am not suggesting that Priestley was sitting at a machine for turning out well-made jokes when he wrote this book, only that in the maturity of his later years he no longer responds to life in exclusively comic terms. He can laugh, yes; and his laughter is honest. But he is not confident that one can search for a true vision through comedy, and this is something it was possible to feel implicit in *The Good Companions*.

In this sense *Festival at Farbridge* could be regarded as a somewhat patronising word of encouragement designed to make a large public feel jollier, and any such case against the book is certainly arguable. The fact remains, however, that it is much funnier than its more successful predecessor, despite occasional fatigue in the writing, one or two inadequate scenes and the awkward burden of two of the central characters. Once again this England, provincial life version, vintage 1951, is from head to toe as true as it could be made, and the book illustrates once more Priestley's powerful gift of balancing social realism with broad comedy. If under stress that comedy turns sometimes into farce and our laughter is clumsily halted, the book is strong enough to support it. It seems possible, if someone takes the trouble to launch the fashion, that *Festival at Farbridge* will eventually slip away from the South-Bank association and stand on its own feet as an extensive and reliable, if somewhat light-weight social portrait of our time viewed in comic terms. The book deserves better than the shrug of dismissal it receives at the moment.

SOME DISTANT WIZARDRY

Before spending a final work-free week-end at Henley that summer, I wanted to take another look at the three remaining works of fiction in Priestley's output since the war. I could remember very little about them beyond the fact that I had found them disappointing—largely, I suspected, for reasons of prejudice. A volume of stories called *The Other Place* was published in 1953, and in the following year came *The Magicians*, so odd and fantastic that it might well have found a place between the same covers. Then, in 1954, *Low Notes on a High Level* was also published.

Apart from the occasional short story buried among the weight of magazines locked and forgotten in the vaults of the thirties, Priestley had always avoided trimming any theory of time or recurrence to fit a work of fiction, possibly because he feared that the weaker disciplines imposed by the novel would allow his imagination to roam too far. This objection cannot be brought so readily against the short stories which require tidiness and point and are never taken too seriously by readers. But *The Magicians* is an attempt to dovetail a realistic novel and a fairy-story, to improve a man's loneliness and dryness of heart by an artificial application of the occult, and that struck me originally, as it did on re-reading the book, as a device which placed too heavy a burden on the reader. On the stage one's reactions are conditioned by the speed at which the dramatist takes the piece; one is at his mercy. But in reading fiction any construction, however taut, gives one time to pause, to drift out of the atmosphere, to lose faith; and this is what happens in *The Magicians*. Into a country-house thick with cigar smoke and financial influences come three wise men, who inform the urbane but embittered industrialist that he must be taught the lesson about the nature of time which Alan Conway divulged to his sister. He falls victim to their insidious spell and is taken back to periods of his life when the fresh winds of youth blew strong and happiness was in the air; he realises his mistakes and determines to profit by them. For this he reaps a suitable reward, arranged by the three mysterious visitants, and the novel ends in the warm comforting glow of a family reunion.

This, we feel, is not life, but an idealised version of existence which has been shamelessly fixed by the novelist. If we accept the grey world of industry, of tired eyes and the breakdown round the corner, then the sepulchral voices of other-worldly creatures droning their messages in foreign accents of the most phoney sort are unlikely to make much of an impression on us. It might be said that the Inspector in *An Inspector Calls* is a being who hails from the same remote sphere as these three men; but he is also unmistakably an inspector, not a third-rate conjuror whose mind is dark with spells, fancies and formulae.

The prejudice that works against me in reading *Low Notes on a High Level* is concerned with the writer's attitude to satire, which is only effective when the scalpel is used with a clinical expressionless face. We must not be conscious that this is a joke at someone's expense, but that the person or institution in question actually exists in this frightening, fatuous and contemptible way. In this book Priestley is poking fun satirically at broadcasting, bureaucracy, lack of imagination in high places and similar matters which have received his more serious and considered criticism in other places. But instead of making his reader squirm with horror and execrate these dangers of our time, Priestley goes for the laughs: his characters have funny names and are involved in comic improbable adventures; the book has an air of fantasy, and he calls it a "frolic". Good observation clears the air of the somewhat cheap laughter that explodes on every page, but one cannot avoid the feeling that a good opportunity for destroying rather than condoning has been lost in the determination to establish an atmosphere of good clean fun. I wished the book had been conceived a little more cruelly.

Despite all this and contrary to what everyone had told me with an assurance only assumed when there is some doubt in the matter, I had found that Priestley's work since the war still struck out in new directions, still tinkered experimentally with his craft, still reached levels of achievement that were, if anything, higher than his performances in the thirties. His best novel was undoubtedly *Bright Day*; his most effective and personal book of essays, which was published in 1949, was *Delight*. No more suitable books to keep beside the bed could be found in those moments when insomnia bites into one's mind and the nights are painful. And perhaps too he had written his best plays since the war: that remained to be seen. Meanwhile the last of autumn required to be watched; the winds were laden with cold rain and hastened the damp leaves down the path from the pub, and I remember thinking one afternoon that this winter would be warmly improved if I went to the theatre more often. One's most decisive resolves always come when a season is on the change.

VIII. A Post-War Dramatist

THE DRAMATIC TIGHTWIRE

THERE came a time when I could put on a better suit, hail a taxi at the corner of Porchester Terrace and drive east to a theatre where one of Priestley's plays was making its first appearance in London. Going to the theatre sharpens one's sense of occasion, stimulates a childlike appetite for life so that even the street-lamps cast a more intense light into the cab, and one therefore expects a great deal from the play, perhaps too much. Quite rightly, too, if the play happens to be serious: one should always expect too much from a work of art and distinguish the great works from the good by finding in them even more than one expected. But of the two plays by Priestley I have seen in recent years, the first, *Mr. Kettle and Mrs. Moon*, asked to be judged purely as entertainment, and the second, *The Glass Cage*, was a stern naturalistic play concerned with the way extreme clashes of temperament wreak havoc as well as work constructively within a family. The comedy enjoyed a long run at the Duchess Theatre, where suburban families chortled nightly for several months; while the other play, specially written to accommodate a talented group of Canadian actors from Toronto, was given a limited season at the Piccadilly.

Both of them I found disappointing, the first because it seemed to be looking back to a vein of comedy and a source of material which Priestley had fully exploited in other work, the second on rather less lazy grounds, that for some reason, even with all its elements sparking and electrically alive, it failed ever to catch fire. In much of Priestley's early work, particularly the novels, we have been exhorted to shuffle off the repressive influences of the mortal coil and find our way to

clearer and more spacious heights of living. The fact that he is
profoundly and simply right, however, does not justify him in
repeating the message so frequently that he gives an overworked
platitudinous ring to his own sayings. In a sense, with *Mr.
Kettle and Mrs. Moon*, he has been guilty of vulgarising material
which at one time, more freshly and naturally reflecting the
shape of his mind, made its effect because he believed it truly,
however ingenuous it seemed. But this latest exponent of the
importance of never falling victim to a routine of dry half-
conscious hours and flabby relationships is saved only by the
superficial boyishness of its humour; beneath the surface one
detects a cynicism, a decision to resuscitate an old and well-
tried way of making people roll in the aisles. I felt that Priestley
lacked any real imaginative response to the play and that
therefore one's laughter could never be intelligent. We were in
a knockabout world in which respectable people suddenly took
to behaving in an eccentric fashion with a view to shooing our
boredom away for an hour. All the right targets were set up—
pompous officials, notions of conventional behaviour and so
forth—and obligingly knocked down. Priestley has so shrewdly
performed these small services to society elsewhere in his work
(and they are the subject for very serious and considered argument in his two chapters of autobiography) that when he
cheapens them to the level of an unsubtle daily-tabloid attack,
it is somewhat hard to join in the spree of belly-laughs, to share
the night-out for the inhibited. As part of his sudden emancipation from trivial worldly cares, Mr. Kettle decides to whip off
Mrs. Moon's spectacles and take her to bed, and the scene is
so deliberately geared for the production of shocked giggles
that one almost feels, in the squirming of the audience, that the
play is on the brink of pornography.

The piece runs so strongly against the current of what
Priestley has always wanted for the theatre that it seems bound
to strike an admirer of his serious plays as practically an act of
betrayal. As I came out of the theatre wrestling with the
problem of where to eat, an historic moment was enacted: for
the first time in my long acquaintance with Priestley's work I

felt a certain sympathy for the coiners of the Jolly Jack legend. And coiners they are, too, for out of base metal they have put a good deal of worthless small change into circulation, which for many years has persuaded people to ignore the handful of sovereigns which Priestley himself has produced. Gold, happily, is indestructible.

It was astonishing that eight years before *Mr. Kettle and Mrs. Moon* the same theatre could have held a play by the same author so gentle, melancholy and strong that by any standard it must be placed high among post-war contributions to the drama. This was *The Linden Tree* which, like *The Glass Cage*, attempts an exploration of family relationships, the revelation of individual people through the awkward balances they strike when involved in a close drama, and the process of extensive inward development in the course of a short outward action. It is the play which displays at its finest Priestley's gift for making his characters deeper and more rounded than the particular situation of the play requires them to be. Yet this is done, not by imparting information irrelevant to the plot, but by means of such a close watch on the timing and construction of the piece that every moment tells you more about the character than the character tells you in the words he uses. This is not merely a question of the implications of character to be found in choice of words, the way a person speaks, his reactions to others; one perceives it rather in the individual atmosphere that rises from each of the people and joins above the detail of scenes and events to make the mood of the play.

Thus, on this more elevated and sensitive plane of mood which Priestley first tried to create in *Eden End*, is to be found the more moving significance of the piece, and talking about it belongs to the same type of critical problem as the effort to state exactly what a poem is about. I could offer a detailed account of the content of *The Linden Tree* and feel when I had finished that I had shifted further from the play's true subject than if I had kept silence.

As I walked the windy garish length of the Strand after *Mr. Kettle and Mrs. Moon* I bitterly regretted that some theory

N

of time could not be put to the practical use of whizzing me
back eight years to that very different Priestley in the same
place. For *The Linden Tree* may be regarded as the centre-piece
of his performance in the theatre since the war, if not as the
best excursion into apparent naturalism he has ever made. It
was produced in 1948, in the middle of Priestley's second concentrated burst of effort to subdue Shaftesbury Avenue to his
pen, and two plays lie on either side of it. *An Inspector Calls*,
after a curious jaunt to Moscow where it was favourably
received in the summer of 1945, reached London more than a
a year later and took its place, even more curiously, as the only
contemporary piece in the Old Vic repertory for that season.
Ever Since Paradise, which must have seemed in the drab metropolitan scene of 1947 a supernaturally joyous and bright-eyed
hangover from the thirties, had been written before the war,
much revised and at last launched on a successful tour of the
provinces in 1946.

Then, after *The Linden Tree* had shown Priestley's concern
for the anxieties of individuals trying to drop anchor in the
rough seas of a changing society, he tried to enlarge his dramatic compass to deal, no less topically, with the greater social
changes that were beginning to rock the world at large. *Home
Is Tomorrow*, set on a Caribbean island where a United Nations
group are attempting with missionary zeal to work towards a
better world, is a study of outlooks, a dramatic glance cast
quickly but intensely over the international scene. And then
in 1950 came *Summer Day's Dream*, a glimpse of the green world
of the South Downs in a quarter of a century's time, urgently
discussing certain values which seemed to Priestley to be
currently imperilled by placing them with their backs to the
wall, at their final moment of crisis.

The problem play, which seeks to perform the first stage in
ironing out a social difficulty by making people sympathetically
aware that the difficulty exists in profoundly human and not
just airily theoretical terms, has been much in vogue since the
war. Playwrights acquired the habit during the late forties of
letting their social consciences loose in prison cells and school

dormitories and revealing some lacuna in the social pattern which everyone thought, hopefully but not very sensibly, the glorious release from world war would have automatically removed. The new and even further-reaching set of problems imposed by the challenging onset of peace thus found their way absorbingly into the theatre, and plays like *The Guinea Pig* and *Now Barabbas* seemed at last to clear the way to getting ideas into the theatre and keeping it popular at the same time.

Priestley succeeded with *The Linden Tree*, by no means a cheering unrationed play, and he enjoyed by far his longest run with it; but *Home Is Tomorrow* perhaps set up house too late in this particular boom-town, for it achieved one of Priestley's most remarkable failures in the commercial theatre. High hopes were held of it. During rehearsals it was felt to be one of his most interesting plays and a spell in the provinces confirmed that impression. But when it came to the Cambridge Theatre in the late autumn of 1948, nobody liked it, and there was an odd and perhaps very revealing divergence of opinion among the critics as to the nature of the play. "One influential critic", Priestley has written, "called it a discussion on a desert island; another said it was not a play at all but a bunch of essays; and yet another announced that I was trying to write a thriller in the John Buchan manner." A piece that is open to such clashing interpretations, even if these views are at fault in themselves, must evidently lack that indefinable demon which enables a play to cross the footlights and make its point quite plain. One has the feeling that the action of *Home is Tomorrow* is proceeding dimly behind a gauze curtain while the dramatist is himself standing illuminated by a spot, wearing workaday clothes and throwing off a few generalisations about world affairs.

I have not seen the play, and I do not know. But reading it suggests to me that the conviction of Priestley's inability to keep the pulpit out of the drawing-room had gained such a hold by now that many people could think of nothing else. If you visit the theatre in the firm belief that you are going to be peppered by a crossfire of arguments, then you will obviously wince every time you hear a blank loosed off five miles away. From reviews of *The Linden Tree* one gains the impression that the piece was so proficient and moving, despite the ideas that underlay it, that the critics were bound by their own desire to avoid seeming foolish to give it the choice words it deserved. But in *Home is Tomorrow* they had an arguable point in suggesting that the balance of power was weighted too heavily in favour of material better suited to a chair of political theory than a plush stall, and perhaps they made the most of it.

I have no wish to throw up a mild echo of Priestley's loud and well-argued grudges against the dramatic critics; I believe on the whole that, except in the rare event of a critic baring his teeth on a personal vendetta, an author receives the kind of critical treatment to which his work, his public personality and his professional manners lay him open. It is one of the penalties of occasionally appearing in front of one's creations, either to display them more effectively or to vouchsafe an announcement on some quite different topic, that one becomes very closely and often incongruously associated with one's work, and judgment is inevitably nudged a little off the perfect dispassionate balance. Everyone knows that Priestley smokes a pipe; children are always disappointed when they discover there is a man with a gnarled face and a drooping cigarette inside the Punch and Judy box.

CHANT THE THEME WOMAN

But a critic who goes to the lengths, as one did, of saying that *Ever Since Paradise* was another instance of solemn preaching must have tottered very happily out of the stalls bar on the night he saw the play and come to with the most wretched headache on the morning of writing his notice. There was no excuse for this. Even the most tedious white-surpliced ecclesiastic will have stopped preaching a sermon, in the accepted sense of the phrase, if he suddenly begins to theorise about sexual relations from the pulpit. It is the only subject about which it is almost impossible to be dull or repetitive, and we

have a childlike appetite for hearing the most fundamental
sexual truths over and over again. Sex is the concern of *Ever
Since Paradise*, and Priestley for the first time escapes from the
inhibitions which haunted his previous attempts to write about
it. And if that were not enough, he had worked out a fresh
emancipation from theatrical convention to give an original
focus to the points he wanted to demonstrate. The play is
fluent, light of touch, full of quick movement and terse comment, making a firework display of something which is usually,
even in comedy, more in the nature of a serious and carefully
planned exhibition.

Ever Since Paradise makes the attempt, in the casual offbeat
way that is more the fashion now than it was, to "create a new
and valuable relationship between players and audience".
Priestley, who in his occasional writing has often made a
symbol out of charades and music halls because they involved
him so deeply in youth, has tried to bring the gaiety and
informality of the charade to the strict cold stage. Pianos, a few
gentle rhythms, quickly relax the audience, and a mood is
established in which anything can be said, as between old
friends. There are six characters; two of them sit at grand
pianos, bicker entertainingly and comment on the action, while
they lazily provide music appropriate to the little dramas they
are watching; a mature married couple, violently opposed in
their theories about love and marriage, command the action
which takes place on an inner stage like a small demonstration
room where the third couple are exhibited in typical scenes
from every stage of their relationship. The scene shifts from
moment to moment, time rushes back and forth, the stage
crackles with activity and controversy, the music tinkles in and
out. The older couple, briskly assuming wigs and accents, act
the parts of in-laws and adulterers, the various influences for
evil and good that creep through a marriage.

The play, apparently so vague in its purpose and direction,
is in fact beautifully constructed, and as it gathers pace and
intensity from its timing and almost contortionist stagecraft
one is swept out of the indolent fireside attention which the

beginning encourages into an excitable concern to discover what happens next and to hear exactly what words will come out of the almost monstrous freedom to comment practised by the characters. If nothing is said about the subject which we did not know before, the vehicle chosen for it is so charming, natural and buoyant that the age-old comedy of sex is refreshed. This play, always more popular on the continent than at home, where, as Ivor Brown says, "the popularity of the ordinary lounge-hall setting and naturalistic performance worked against it", would be more than likely to succeed if it were revived in these days of a theatre less firmly entrenched in the narrow three-act routines which impoverished the drama creatively between the wars. For the experiment in *Ever Since Paradise* enabled the stage to accommodate, not just the play of character committed to situations and events, but the free expression of personality at large within a broad subject. Shaw only just succeeds by sheer brilliance in making art out of the pure freedom of conversation; he cancelled the effect of statements that were individually important because he left them dramatically unsatisfactory. Priestley at least found the craft for the task.

TO ASK SOME QUESTIONS

An Inspector Calls joins hands over the years with *Dangerous Corner*, for it is a return to the same method, the thriller that closes breathlessly on an unexpected twist of time's tail. Unity of time and place hold it intensely together, and the action is continuous. We enter as the Birling family, as prosperous, smug and unshakeable as the people in Priestley's first play seemed to be, are celebrating an engagement; a treacly atmosphere of congratulation thickens the air even more densely than the cigar smoke. Into their midst, however, comes the Inspector, a formal uncompromising figure armed with such shrewd questions and relentless determination to achieve the truth that he forces from every member of the family the kind of admission that displays their character in depth. His enquiry concerns a girl who committed suicide, and it slowly and uncomfortably emerges that they have all in one way or another contributed to the causes of her death. The father sacked her for demanding more money; the daughter complained about her manners to a shop manageress and insisted on her dismissal; the mother refused to allow her charitable committee to help the girl financially when she was expecting a child; and the son of the family was that child's father. Uneasy, frightened, the family are left alone to rake over the dry bones of their self-satisfaction. As the realisation dawns on them that perhaps the visit was a hoax (the Inspector shows them each a photograph, but they might all have been looking at different girls), the ground is cleared for a moral battle. Only the son and daughter recognise that according to a spiritual standard of truth they are still responsible, while the others with brusque irritability start fighting their way back to self-esteem. When they are fully satisfied that the Inspector was an impostor and the curtain is about to fall, the telephone rings: a girl, having swallowed disinfectant, is dying in hospital and a police inspector is on his way to make a few enquiries.

Priestley has no sense of personal sin but strong feelings of social responsibility; for him, the eyes of God do not exist but one must avoid, by adherence to the strictest code of morality, putting out the eyes of one's neighbour. *An Inspector Calls*, written quickly and with that passionate concern to brush aside pretences and plunge neck-high into the truth which distinguishes so much of Priestley's work, is a play so tightly constructed and fiercely pursued that the moral force behind it smacks almost of the inquisition. Priestley seems determined to torture these people with their social crimes, to have them damned even before their responsibility is proved. Because they might be guilty of inducing a helpless girl to take her life, then they must be exposed and ripped to pieces. The impact is merciless, and Priestley's brand of writing for the theatre, which is more clear than eloquent, cut hard with a knife rather than fashioned soft by the hands, is ideally suitable to this type of play which proceeds with the irrefutable logic of an argument.

For this reason the play is convincing. The complaint that
Priestley has almost wrenched the long arm of coincidence
from its socket—it is most improbable that all these people
would have been involved with the girl—is answered not only
by the point about the photographs, but by the fact that it
makes no difference to the dramatic intensity whether we know
who the girl is, where the Inspector really came from or, for
that matter, what particular religious ethic happens to be
supported by Priestley's intention. All this is irrelevant; all we
are meant to see, and we should be moved by it to an examination of our own motives, principles and honesty, is a vision of
the solemn responsibility involved in being a member of human
society. We are not alone, and we cannot act with an insolent
disregard of others. The incidents chosen to illustrate this
theme might break the rules of coincidence in a purely naturalistic play, but here they are appropriate to the theme and
typical of the characters in the slightly formalised way that a
true assessment of Priestley's purposes empowers one to accept.
The production of a film which used realistic flashback to
enliven the action may have guaranteed the public a good
thriller, but it dissipated the intensity and removed the peculiar
quality of the play.

An Inspector Calls suited Moscow well immediately after the
war, and it was given simultaneous production at two important
theatres. New York, Paris and other European capitals were
swift to bring it to their stages and, like a number of Priestley's
plays, it has always captured more applause abroad than at
home. From Scandinavia, Central Europe, the Low Countries,
requests for performing rights are never off his agent's desk; it
would be safe to guess from the astonishing figures that the
curtain has gone up on *Dangerous Corner* more times and in more
places than any other play written during the past thirty years.
One or two plays, like *An Inspector Calls*, have been snatched
across the Channel before any English management could be
found for them—this was the case with *Take the Fool Away*
which opened in Vienna in 1956 but still lies between manuscript covers in this country. None of this is to say that the

English theatre has been ungrateful to Priestley, for in view of his refusal to take root in one particular corner he has collected a very reasonable number of successes.

From a commercial point of view a restless nature serves a writer much less reliably than fierce concentration on a solitary line of development, for in each new experiment he is wandering back to the anxious steps and sometimes naïve mistakes of an artistic childhood and once again he must break down another exhibition of parental resistance from conservative audiences. It is as though the child irritated everyone by never finally making up his mind what he wanted to be when he grew up. Fortunately for the liveliness of his work, Priestley has never grown up in this respect, although there are occasions when one regrets the impatience that prevents him from following up an interesting innovation that perhaps failed because only the writing and staging of it could teach him the mistakes to avoid.

A case in point is *Dragon's Mouth*, the dramatic quartet which he wrote with Jacquetta Hawkes in 1950, which was an attempt to prise the stuff of drama even further away from the conventions of the stage: thus to preserve its unique value, which is so closely tied in with actually going to a theatre and joining the body of an audience, from the depredations of radio and television. Requiring no set and virtually no movement, this play pared down the essential elements of theatre to the basis of live actors speaking live words on a stage; and the responsibility for creating the genuine communal illusion was taken away from the usual paraphernalia of scenery and plot and placed on the imagination of the audience—an audience, thought Priestley, trained by radio to form the pleasurable image through the ear, yet still needing something alive but not kicking to occupy the eye. But "I cannot bear waiting long for anything good to happen. I have never been able to plan far ahead, to settle today what I shall be doing in two or three years' time. I rush at anything—even work." And having rushed once, he retires breathless but undaunted to cast about for another apparently insuperable difficulty to challenge him. Priestley has been a commissionaire of the theatre, opening

unexpected doors and windows to release some of the stuffy air
and let in the light at strange tantalising angles, but he lacks
the persistence that can turn a sudden original flare into the
strong steady light of a new way of doing things.

A KIND OF LONG FAREWELL

I do not say that he never develops a branch of his art or returns
to explore more thoroughly a form or manner he has tried
before. When he does so the result has a technical virtuosity,
because he writes with the ease of complete independence from
the problems of the form, which leaves him free to concentrate
on the deepening of more serious material. The Inspector
might have called less confidently if the dangerous corner had
not been already turned, and certainly *The Linden Tree* owes a
good deal to its predecessor in the same gentle pastel-shaded
genre of dramatic understatement, *Eden End*. It is not an
experimental play, it contains no surprises, it is neatly constructed in three acts with good curtain lines and dramatic
exchanges; and it drew audiences to the Duchess for more than
a year. If Priestley had confined his interest to this type of
straightforward realism in which emotions are slanted like an
innuendo and, though delivered in a manner as clipped as a
military moustache, suggest worlds of feeling to an English
audience, Priestley would almost certainly be accepted as the
leading naturalistic playwright of our time. As it is, he is never
called the leading playwright of anything. He is the dramatist
who, like the time he represents and tries to speak for, went his
own unpredictable and often dangerous way.

One thinks of the low-hanging branches of a linden tree
brushed by a melancholy wind and although no symbolism
was intended in the title, that particular tree carries a fair
suggestion of the atmosphere of the piece. To have called the
family Birch, for example, would have been out of key with the
play. In varying forms the Lindens had been with Priestley for
many years; before the war in Arizona he had begun a play
with the same title that also tried to perform the so fragile task

of establishing a family mood, but had broken off half-way through because it was "not like me at all and might have been a play written by somebody else". It is possible that the drift of feeling which Priestley had failed to pin down in that earlier attempt stayed with him as the vaguest but still potent memory during the war, and then, enriched by new attitudes, emerged in this different guise. For once again, and even more strongly than ever, the characters of this play have the gift of making us feel that we have known them before and have come to the theatre really in order to discover what has been happening to them.

Two conflicts greet us. The Professor who has for many years held the chair of history at this provincial university is about to be forcibly retired and he is protesting, not so much against being thrown out, but because he feels that the new policy they are pursuing and the new people they are appointing are wrong, destructive and uncivilised. At the same time his home is the scene of a family reunion: a daughter returns from her wealthy marriage in the hot indolent landscapes of France, a son drives slickly down from London and horrifies the Professor with his offhand boasting of somewhat underhand success, another daughter comes from her London hospital crisp with progressive ideas. Only the youngest girl who has remained at home still relaxes under the pretty Edwardian parasol of culture and refinement which has shaped the Professor's standards all his life and which now, in the aching disappointment of change, turns his mind back to Ranji and Maclaren batting at Lord's on summer afternoons, to a society that gave him peace because of the imperceptibly fading beauty, like a slant of evening sunshine, that is to be found in any established order.

The Professor is one of Priestley's most affecting characters, for he has come to the bitterness of knowing that his wisdom and quiet love for this world have no power to restrain or mitigate the irresponsibility with which the young new world, of which his children seem at first sight the vulgar fanfares, is coming into being. Yet the emotion of regret, so apparently tender and feeble to act, is a creative force, and out of it the

Professor gains the rare philosophic heights that take a person
beyond time's reach and thus enable him to discover with
sympathy the reasons why the present seems to be casting such
an alien spell on things and people he holds dear. He fights to
give a pattern to disorder, and in doing so, after some jagged
and painful breaks, he succeeds in drawing his family closer
about him. His is the bewildered eye through which a changing
society is viewed, analysed and finally understood; and his
children are the guinea-pigs of that society, each of them
representing a typical post-war reaction and displaying the
dangers that particularly threaten a world in need of red blood
and a hard-headed courage.

Priestley is able to make his points covertly, burying them in
undertones that murmur consistently throughout the piece,
because he does not take sides. His sympathies bridge the gulf
of years which yawns between the family attitudes and he
tries to show dramatically how valid and explicable they are.
He proves again in this play that he is one of the few authors
who have never suffered from the middle-aged complaint of
slackening sympathies, of lagging behind the years. He knows
that a stroke played by Hutton at Lords in 1948 is in no way
less magical than the roar that greeted a boundary from Ranji
forty years before; he knows that the sun can still entrance a
landscape in a haze of permanence. Because of this he continues to fight on all fronts that defend his beliefs, and *The
Linden Tree* constitutes one of the major victories. A shrewd
glance at the present should always have the effect of extending
one's vision back to the past and forward to the future, and it is
no doubt one of the by-products of Priestley's obsession with the
nature of time that he has been empowered to do this.

As Priestley pointed out, this play opened no magic casements; it offered material as drab and uncomfortable as the
leather chairs in a senior common-room. But the effect, in a
London trying to breathe in the indecisive post-war vacuum,
was uplifting, partly on account of the confidence with which
Priestley thrust out his jaw (this was the last time he could unite
an audience by appealing to their sense of common danger),

and partly because the action, despite the quarrels and raw nerves that keep it moving, is lit by a gleam of melancholy beauty that fades and brightens through the piece like incidental music. Audiences, too, always like to become acquainted with a family; they are put at ease by watching variations on relationships—between father and child or husband and wife—the basic nature of which they instinctively understand. When they are faced with more sophisticated affairs, as between titled lady and lover in *Home is Tomorrow*, the dramatist's task becomes harder, not because the English are resistant to infidelity but simply that they do not find it so naturally moving.

ABOLISH ALL FIESTAS

The focus of the two plays that followed *The Linden Tree* was switched on to the future and the practical difficulties of dealing with it, and although the problems discussed and illustrated are all human ones, they are allowed so close to the surface of the play that they tend to turn the people into puppets acting at their command. This is especially irritating in view of some incisive, even witty characterisation that went into *Home is Tomorrow*; one feels that these people might be excitingly alive if only Priestley would let them off duty for a spell. When the plot of a three-act play turns on a native rising it is somewhat difficult to avoid the melodrama of shots fired and messengers panting on stage with the latest bulletins, and this gives an almost comic slant to issues that the dramatist is taking very seriously indeed. The play has wit, it changes mood and tempo as briskly as a folk-dance medley, people are brought from every corner of the world to provide the cast: perhaps, for coherence of effect, it is too much the mixture as never before, too much the cocktail that just fails to blend.

A writer is labouring against heavy odds if he decides to describe a mixed bag of expatriates, for they are not only uprooted and neurotically uncertain of their step, but they cannot be expected to form a satisfactorily involved society when the interests that bind them are mainly official rather than personal. Love interest is thrown into the cocktail like a cherry, but neither Priestley nor his audience considers it more than mildly stimulating. No, American writers all over Europe are daily proving, as their epic novels of café-tables are rejected by the hundredweight, that there is never much to say about the rootless unless they happen to be conducting an intense personal search. Even Larry in *The Razor's Edge* never quite struggled free of his ties. We are an insular people and often will not even try to understand the impulses underlying the more cosmopolitan standards required by our time; a considerable fear lies at the back of it. It is significant that Graham Greene, whose religion is strong enough in the world to act as a kind of spiritual passport to anyone holding it, is almost the only English novelist who is able to strike his roots deep in a foreign country and place a novel there; this does not include novels of war when all the world is uprooted.

Even in Canada, I felt as I came out of *The Glass Cage* on a warm spring evening, Priestley never found the slippered ease which makes his English plays so effortlessly true to their origins in life. He is a writer much more deeply involved in society than in the individual, more concerned with the moves in the game of chess than with the microscopic grain in the wood of which the pieces are made. Despite his quick eye for picking out the essentials of atmosphere and pattern in any society through which he travels (his writing about America in the chapters of autobiography is notable for this), he is bound to be at his most assured in depicting, conveying and criticising the society of which he himself has long been a vocal and observant member.

His novels never dig deep, they sweep horizons. His plays, though they strike further into individual natures, only do so in order to improve the clarity of the position people occupy in relation to one another, and one play, *An Inspector Calls*, was written to make this point explicit once and for all. Mutual responsibility must be even less willingly sacrificed than personal integrity, although in the morally balanced society towards which we are striving the two could never clash. At the same time, while we are encouraged to concentrate on the larger picture, the family or the crowd or the nation, and find our place in its convoluted design, Priestley never forgets the uniqueness of the individual human being which finally puts him beyond the comforts of society into the cell of his own isolation; his attempt to disprove this in *Music at Night* had a formal logic suitable to his dramatic purpose, but it seemed to run contrary to his own instincts. Priestley observes most clearly and comments most effectively when he descends through a wider vision of society to a more minute consideration of particular individuals, so that we see them placed and rooted and surrounded by the chaos of life before we get to know them intimately. In *Time and the Conways*, for example, the family circle is busily established before the individuals begin to emerge. But when he begins with a person and then tries to evoke him by means of internal exploration and building an environment round him, as in *Johnson Over Jordan*, then he is apt to fall victim to the expression of vaguely human aspirations, the conventional hopes and fears which we all share but which banish any trace of individuality from a character. There are no lone-wolves in Priestley, and no true heroes.

More recently Priestley has turned to television in his instinctive efforts to capture the attention of a large audience as well as to satisfy the usual urgent need to chance his arm in a new medium. But it seems unlikely that his contribution to the theatre will be left at that. When he next brings the occasion of a first night to Shaftesbury Avenue, I shall go to it.

IX. A Critic of His Time

I END, a copy of *Thoughts in the Wilderness* lying on the bedside table, in the Isle of Wight one autumn day. After breakfast, one stood on the upper terrace for a while in warm blinding sunlight. Priestley was talking about Bradford where I had been to give a lecture; all that he remembered from the old days before the first war had either faded altogether or been sharpened by imagination into the humours of *The Good Companions*, the moods so briefly glimpsed in *Delight* or the deeper spiritual weathers of *Bright Day*. A little later I had turned and glanced down the gloom of the corridor to see Priestley seated at the piano, wearing a blue beret and smoking a pipe, playing a progression of chords that he recalled from Cambridge after the first war, some incidental music someone had written for the *Oresteia* that depended on sharpening the B flat in the key of E flat major. In bed the night before I had read in *Thoughts in the Wilderness* of Priestley's last encounter with Arnold Bennett, in a crowd jostling out of the Queens' Hall after Toscanini had been conducting Beethoven. And Bennett had cried in his queer staccato high-pitched fashion: "Gives us—a lift—doesn't it?" Then Priestley stood up from the piano, took a stick, lit another pipe, and there was the walk before lunch. It was a day like the perfect measured development of a slow movement, giving the impression of not shifting at all but only changing beyond the influence of time. It gave one a lift.

Thoughts in the Wilderness had been appearing in the *New Statesman* at irregular intervals for some time; they were essays which took an aspect of the modern world and worried it into a focus in which its more alarming significance could be displayed. Once or twice in the course of them Priestley had touched explicitly on the threat of the hydrogen bomb and the dangerous absurdity of the arms race. But he had not yet mounted the public platform of the campaign for nuclear disarmament which took its first impulse from a long, forthright and well-argued piece which he wrote for the *New Statesman* in the early months of 1958. The evening before the walk we took on that hazy motionless day in the Isle of Wight, Priestley had been talking of the possibility of setting such a campaign in motion, and I remember thinking then that the careful piece he was planning to embrace his arguments would have the effect of widening the horizons and violently emphasising the import of the essays he had previously contributed to the *New Statesman*. It was the climax to his anxious, sometimes bitter but always responsible thinking during the past few years, possibly the last and certainly the loudest cry from the wilderness.

The volume which collected these pieces, however, appeared before this climax was reached, and the urgent warnings that catch fire in its pages, the admonitory fingers that are raised, probably aroused less sympathy among readers of the *New Statesman* than they do now, when the book has been published for some time and the country is more electrically conscious of the impossible times which have befallen it. Once again, people might feel as they turned to the gentler and more adult urbanities of Books in General, Priestley has put on his mask of severity, melodramatic and overpainted, to bellow his prophecies of an imminent doomsday. Was it not rather like Wells who assumed, in *Mind at the End of its Tether*, that because he was in his closing years, so was the world? And was Priestley content with merely foretelling the end of civilised society? No: he also insisted on shouting the news in loud simple language, as though we were all foreigners or children, people too much entangled in the idiocies of our private lives to notice what was happening around us. It was all very irritating and just what you might expect from a man with a grudge, an oversize chip on his shoulder.

There is no chip or grudge, however—none large enough, at

o

least, to call the tune when Priestley is piping out these warnings. He admits that he is a vain man, but he is neither con-
ceited nor proud; and vanity is skin-deep. He often enjoys
making a fuss in print about the way his work is publicly
treated, thus ensuring perhaps that it will be handled with even
less justice and respect than formerly, but it is wrong to suppose
that his vision is poisoned by any such deeply embittered
egomania. His manner can often be irritating and apparently
self-centred, his voice too loud, too stridently persuasive. But
he is right in thinking that the wilderness is a long way off for
most people, and we need therefore to be summoned into it, the
better to share the lucid sanity with which he views the perspective of current events, attitudes and lunacies. And in getting this perspective into focus, he is not pricked by the wounded
conceit of an author, but moved by the deep anxieties of a man.

In reprinting these pieces between hard covers Priestley was
troubled lest "polemical pieces, originally written to challenge
and provoke the readers of a weekly review" should seem too
crude, "as if a man were shouting in a drawing-room". If anything, however, the opposite is true; since they were first
published times have changed a little, we are more sharply
aware of the problems of living in a confused democracy. We
are all beginning to echo the same words, cry the same warnings to one another. In fact it looks very much as though the
wilderness contains many more bewildered thoughtful faces
than it did even a year or two years ago.

This wilderness has been a retreat of Priestley's for a long
time, for he has never been apt to espouse any broad inclusive
policy which, once established, loses the flexibility required by
those who wish to be free to change their minds on individual
points when circumstances change. In political discussion his
mind roams from left to right, picking what he wants from
either side, never committing himself for long to a party line.
He is convinced of the inadequacy of what he calls Block
Thinking: "neat sets of beliefs and opinions are fastened together; and you are expected to take the lot."

A man who is thus on the outside of every sphere, political, social, moral or literary, but a man who is none the less far from being an outsider, is in a position to avoid the outbursts of negative complaint which pass for criticism in a democratic society. He is sufficiently independent, far enough removed from it yet at the same time inextricably involved, to undertake the burden of positive criticism; to court unpopularity thereby; but to set us angrily thinking. He can observe with clarity, assess with a judgment that is fresh and unattached, and make his counter-suggestions in an audible voice. This is what Priestley does. He has been doing it for years, but never more urgently than now. The red herrings of an awkward unpredictable personality are often drawn across these *Thoughts in the Wilderness*; behind them, however, there is virtue, humanity and wisdom, dashed off with vigour and a thick-nibbed pen, sometimes so rough and ready that one is tempted to accuse him, before thinking, of banality or boyish impudence, but always harshly snapping his fingers at any traces of complacency in the reader's mind.

SEND DOWN YOUR ROOTS

Priestley is preaching, of course: that has always condemned him. But does it now? He is writing a volume of openly polemical essays, in which both the thought and the language are violent and to the point. In the absence of any sermons worth hearing in the churches, he is busy—other writers please copy, for we need it now—trying to stimulate our deep need for something to believe in, our basic faith in the goodness of life, our determination to think and fight our way out of the senseless, confused, undignified and inhuman predicament. In 1949 Priestley wrote a play, *Summer Day's Dream*, which despite warm audiences and an appreciative press achieved only fifty performances at the St. Martin's Theatre. Running costs were enormously high at a time when conditions were such that only capacity booking would have ensured a long success for the play. But was there another reason for its relative failure? It is worth examining here, for it was Priestley's first wounded and

o*

worried cry of warning, that we should look to our withering
laurels and see things clearly again, after the fall of the first
atom-bombs in Japan had given the world new opportunities
for despair and destruction.

The action of the play is set in 1975, but its atmosphere, as
the title suggests, is that of a dream, a magic of present and past
times established in a nightmare of the future. England has
been devastated in an atom-war and the few people left on the
island have returned to a simple fulfilled life of farming, barter-
ing, tasting their leisure and making their own amusement.
World power, meanwhile, has been divided between Russia
and America, and these two countries are vying peaceably with
each other in the race for material progress. To a quiet decay-
ing mansion on the South Downs come a breakneck American
administrator, a single-minded Indian scientist and a stiff
young Russian woman in the service of her state. They have
been surveying the local hills with a view to setting up on them
international factories for synthetic products, and their heli-
copter has broken down. They are taken into the cream of life
which rises from the simple ways of this English backwater;
they are taught to see the subtlety of the summer weather, to
listen to birds and smell the night flowers; they are forced into
realising how much wiser are the slow ways, the life close to the
land, than the hectic soul-destroying spin of the world which
has caught them up in its futile speed. Their sense of duty and
responsibility—but to what and to whom?—is too heavy for
them and they do not stay to share this rhythmic and deeply
satisfying life, but at least they agree to leave it as it was when
they came.

Priestley constructed this play with great skill, so that its
atmosphere, which is a more persuasive advocate than direct
argument of the simple point he wishes to triumph, is not only
conveyed by speech which has very little recourse to direct
poetic evocation, but also manages to grow stronger and more
heady as the action proceeds. By the end the feeling of summer
is as powerful as the scent of orange blossom or the tender
appeal of the music which weaves, with perfect dramatic

justification, through the final act. Each of the English characters contributes to this atmosphere and thereby adds to the
weight of the argument: the old man hovering in final peace
of mind on the threshold of death, the middle-aged widow
with her mystical moments of intuition, the son who works on
the farm and composes music, the bright daughter who writes
poetry. They are all living deeply within this dream, yet their
forthright and unaffected talk, their blunt refusal to compromise with the gods of science and invention, give them also a
stark reality which Priestley cleverly emphasises at the expense
of the unreality of synthetic products, world plans, busy lives
dominated by the gadgets and speed-machines of modern
civilisation. The people are real, and therefore the dream is
real. The three visitors have been living parched and unreal
lives, but for a moment they are touched into humanity,
brought face to face with the basic standards of the only truly
happy life that human beings can make. The primitive peoples
are the wise ones; the super-civilised are going mad. How can
we possibly need reminding?

And yet we do. Often, in this beautiful, humorous and
unsentimental play, Priestley puts into the mouths of his three
uneasy foreigners the anxieties and frustrations, some of them
very small, which bother all of us. It is easier, in fact—and one
should feel guilty at the thought—to identify one's hurried
urban life in 1958 with the lives of those foreigners than with the
quiet pastoral dream which they reject. When the American
speaks of the hollow place, right bang in the middle of things,
one knows too well what he means: "the big dead spot, the
ash-can a thousand miles deep where nothing moves, nothing
grows, nothing lives." This is the Something Else on which
Priestley tries to put his finger in *Thoughts in the Wilderness*, "the
faint but persistent unease, the feeling that experience falls
short of expectation". We are all troubled by it more or less,
particularly if we live in a city, especially if our lives, running
with the stream, turn out to be something snatched, as it were,
between meals. We have no time for a faith to be satisfied. Yet
if sometimes we pause, we can be captured by an experience

which does not lack the Something Else. The Dawlish family in *Summer Day's Dream* had been forced back on their own resources and on those of the fertile land, and they had stumbled on a way of life in which the hollow centre had been permanently filled; they wanted nothing more than the little they had. Priestley himself describes one such moment of complete satisfaction when, late at night, he sat over a dying fire and listened to a record of Schubert's Quintet in C. In such times and conditions as these the wilderness does not appear to exist at all, although in fact one is probably even further into it than ever.

The "hollow place" had its original centre in America, and in one of his pieces called "Our New Society" Priestley indicates that the politicians' lack of guiding vision as to the kind of Britain that needed to be created after the war has been partly responsible for the growth of the transatlantic influence in these islands. As we bow more and more before the high winds of "progress" from across the ocean, so we become less and less rooted in a society specifically our own. Under the uneasy influence of a foreign drug, we are losing our identity. In the course of that essay Priestley mentions a book which was designed to throw this very serious problem into relief: *Journey Down a Rainbow*, written in collaboration with his wife, Jacquetta Hawkes, and published in 1955.

CARING LIKE CRAZY

They travelled to the States together, but at Kansas City their paths diverged. Jacquetta Hawkes went to Albuquerque, where among the Indians of New Mexico she hoped to discover a living example of civilisation as it was when the earliest inhabitants of the continent made their home there. Priestley, just across the state line into Texas, chose the most violent contrast in the shape of two cities, Dallas and Houston, which "are for their size the richest and most rapidly expanding cities in the western world". They did not set out deliberately to prove a theory, though the point of the work must have been in their minds, hoping to be proved, when they planned the expedition. They merely wanted, as much for artistic as for sociological reasons, to place side by side two very different ways of life, dispassionately observed and honestly reported, and leave the reader to make whatever judgment seemed to him fair. By any absolute standard Jacquetta Hawkes keeps her side of this bargain more temperately than Priestley keeps his. She found herself among a people whose instinctive usages and daily routines had been subjected to the test of time and emerged unscathed into the modern age; and they were a people to whom she naturally responded. She therefore visited them with a slight but unsentimental bias in their favour, and that is a better basis for detached observation than the slight but aggressive bias against the steel-bound world of slot-machines and fast cars which Priestley, being the man he is, must have felt when he moved into Dallas and Houston. Her prose is quiet, subtle and rhythmic; she can afford to rely on more discreet metaphors to make her effects; her point of view appears to her to be so much in line with what it is obviously right and natural to think of the civilisation of the Indians that no grand effort of eloquence is required to get it across to the reader. But if she confines her statements to the resources of a string quartet, Priestley masses a full orchestra of sound to launch his devastating attack on the modern side of the border. In none of his work can one readily detect the dispassionate observer at work, for his words always roar across the full-throated page like trumpets, as though the emotional impact of what he has seen has released a flood of language to distort the true picture. That is sometimes the effect, particularly when Priestley has written out of a deep concern. He is anxious not to be misunderstood; he is worried lest one ounce of the force of the scenes he has observed should be lost between him and the reader, and for that reason he pitches his language high, choosing vast images and monumental comparisons. His voice must be loud, not to drown the frantic noise of, for instance, the juke-boxes and the football, but at least to match it. Where the impressions are violent, so must be the words; and that means, as far as convincing the reader is concerned, that he loses on the roundabouts of apparent prejudice what he gains on the swings of force and clarity.

Thus, at first sight, the book seems unbalanced. The woman, a restrained scientific witness already involved in the study of ancient cultures, goes to the world she is likely to comprehend sympathetically, and reports it in her fluent, delicate prose. The man, a highly trained journalist with an imaginative and somewhat ferocious eye, visits the places which he must know in advance he will dislike, for he shares her conviction of the fundamental simplicity of life. But it is precisely because they do share this conviction, and in their different ways can voice it with equal eloquence, that the book on second thoughts recovers its balance and begins to take the full strain of its meaning. One realises that the ways of the Indians make just the same impression, gentle and integrated and fulfilled, as Jacquetta Hawkes's prose, while Priestley's hasty vigorous sentences are an ideal mirror to reflect the full horror of what is happening in the fast-expanding cities of the west. Fundamentally their beliefs have the same weight and direction: they agree in their conclusions. And there is little to choose between them in the sharpness and honesty with which they approached their subjects. They are both, in this book, very serious writers indeed. Allowing for differences of manner and temperament, one feels that their facts would have emerged in much the same pattern if they had changed places that night in Kansas City when their ways parted.

This is a very valuable, civilised and disturbing book, for even if we were aware of the variety and potency of the influences that crawl deeper into our society with every ship and aircraft that arrives from New York, it is hard to estimate the extent of that influence, and the possible damage it could do, unless it is occasionally brought to our notice in an extreme form. That is the value of *Journey Down a Rainbow*; that is why it disturbs. We are shown an almost ludicrously exaggerated version, the logical extreme, of the changes that have been

taking place in our own cities during the past twenty years.
And we are shown it in contrast to a placid portrait of the type
of civilisation, in atmosphere if not in detail, at which we
should really be aiming. Jacquetta Hawkes has reported a
society that exists today, which in its essence bears a close
resemblance to the dreaming yet down-to-earth society that
Priestley foretold for England after an atom-war in *Summer
Day's Dream*. That play was a dramatic fiction at which one
could laugh, by which one might be charmed or diverted. The
book, however, sticks to the facts. Yet the two works say the
same thing; and they are equally real.

So we are still in the wilderness, and on every side there is a
menace of unpredictable power and influence closing in on us.
Such thoughts as these are heavy and dramatic; they avoid the
subtleties of living on this earth and take the direct route to
the obvious and most plangent statement; they are the stuff of
sermons that cannot be preached too often; they have been
Priestley's concern, more with an eye for reality than an instinct
for prophecy, for several years. He has tried to make art out of
them, and he has come artlessly into the open. As with so many
of his contemporaries, a concern that was social and insular in
the thirties has broadened into a vision of what is happening in
the world at large, and it is even more apparent now than
before that by the most violent means at his disposal, by using
his craft and yoking his imagination to the task, he has always
tried in his work to urge and move people to a consideration
of their private lives in the public setting of their time, their
society and the dark influences that seem beyond their individual control.

In the course of a career of responsible social criticism in
which he has never seen fit to lower his voice or pull his
punches, Priestley has made enemies. For some he has been too
obvious, for others, in whom his personality sets up no familiar
echo, he has behaved egocentrically in his writing, cut too
much of a dash. He has written and said a great deal about
himself, for he is always fair to his reader in the sense that he
sets his thoughts and feelings in the context of his own character,

so that due allowance may be made for that. He has hit back perhaps too often when those enemies attack him, and by denying it he has tended to add to the legend of a man who enjoys nothing, is never satisfied and cannot for a moment stop complaining. For reasons like these many people sentenced him to the wilderness long before he chose to go there himself. But the hermit is worth a visit. He may have a wise word or two to say, if one is patient.

Where, he asks, are the clowns and drolls who could dissolve into laughter much that is bitterly frustrating now? What is the essence of that curious experience which happens when, wheezing a bit, heavy with food and drink, he waddles along the hall, switches on the set, drops into his chair and puts his feet up, then peers into his magic mirror like a fourteen-stone cigar-smoking Lady of Shalott? Are we not rapidly arriving at a time when masses of people do not really want anything until they are told they want it? Where now are all the glorious old Insider Artists, who were the ordinary men of their time writ large, who created out of an abundance of energy and joy, who praised God for all their fellows? Do we live in fact in a world of doers who also ask us—or compel us—to regard them as seers? Are we between two vast and powerful societies that are governed, each in its own way, by the masculine principle not reasonably balanced by the feminine? What must we do, how should we act, in what way can things be changed? The hermit, conscious that he cannot hold our butterfly attention for long, expands into anecdote, narrows into analysis, bursts into pyrotechnic generalisation, constantly changes tempo, shifts his stance, offers another point of view. Even if we are there to scorn him, it is difficult not to listen; his voice is loud but well-modulated and his shafts are intended to provoke. If we are there merely to be entertained, he will amuse us. He has always been a good hand at holding our interest.

JUST ONE WORD MORE

Summer Day's Dream in 1949 may be taken as a lazy semi-poetical fantasy, to pass an evening in a pleasant haze as we watch the resolution of a number of dramatic situations. *Journey Down a Rainbow*, six years later, can be read and enjoyed as the vigorous work of two attractive travellers who keep their eyes open. *Thoughts in the Wilderness*, published as a whole in 1957, need only be regarded at its lowest as a virtuoso display of ideas, prejudices and reflections. But depending on the angle from which one is inclined to view Priestley's writing, these three works, so different in form but so similar in theme and uniformly urgent in their undercurrents of concern, may be judged as the climax to a lifetime of "engaged" literary production. The craft and cunning that succeed in containing a broad sweep of vision in simply constructed sentences have grown even more effective; his imagination is unimpaired, his human sympathy is still as warm as when *The Good Companions* flowed out of it. "We must think freshly, think fast, improvise, experiment, and be tolerant of one another's mistakes": so he writes in *Thoughts in the Wilderness*. Priestley himself has never been notably tolerant, but his thoughts have been fresh and fast, he has constantly changed his methods, broken new ground, and explored territory unknown to him.

The rules for writing plays which he lays down in a stimulating lecture called *The Art of the Dramatist*, published in 1957, can certainly be favourably applied to his own drama and might also be adapted to reflect his attitude to every branch of his colossal and various output. The dramatist must work simultaneously on two different levels, to bring life into the Theatre, and the Theatre into life; Priestley has always regarded art as an integral part of life, not an abstraction or merely an expression of it. They feed each other, richly. Secondly, the dramatist should think in terms of action; the talk should always be moving towards an action. Very rarely, except in the early essays, has he permitted himself to indulge in talk for its own sake; he moves back to people and human situations all the time, to enlighten the former by illuming the latter. Next the dramatist should have a continuous and varied series of little dramas within his big drama. Priestley is a writer broad enough in vision to allow his work, particularly in fiction, to digress into the revealing detail of life without taking his eye off the main purpose, the essential theme. Then, the dramatist should suggest life going on beyond his scenes. Only a writer who keeps very close to life, who does not withdraw himself to a higher realm of art where the air is rarefied, can do this, and at a time when so much art appears to exist in the vacuum of the artist's unconscious mind, this has been one of Priestley's major virtues. The dramatist should aim at a constant slight surprise throughout his scenes, but in his main theme he should arouse and then satisfy the expectation of his audience. Priestley, especially in his early work, is adept at suggesting the oddness and eccentricity of the human scene without distracting the reader's sympathy from a central situation with which he can identify himself. Finally, just as the dramatist must look for new life on one level, so he should experiment on the other level, of theatrical form and style, to discover what best expresses that life and the bent of his mind. Priestley's mind, ranging and exploratory, has always attempted to extend his work in both these senses, and while this accounts for some of his failures, it has also ensured that he has never fallen into the lifeless repetition, the marking time, which can make an artist seem like a somewhat melancholy hangover from a previous generation.

Books which end with a summary, however, are admitting defeat. If the matter could be effectively summarised, why extend it to the length of a book? If it cannot, what is the point of destroying the mood in which the long journey has been undertaken by supplying an unsupported outline of the essentials? I have no wish to draw conclusions: only to set down within a chapter of autobiography certain thoughts that have occurred to me during an acquaintance with the work of J. B. Priestley lasting several years. His books and plays are not set within a precise pattern of merit, according to critical

standards carefully set forth. I have often spent more time on
work that was below his best, and my interest at a particular
moment, in certain circumstances, has been the only guide to
which I have listened. I recall, therefore, that deckchair in the
sun, that afternoon when I tried to defeat a headache by sliding
deep into a book, the night when I stayed awake waiting for a
telephone call, the boat that fought the North Sea hour after
hour, as one sat with a book on one's knee, turning page after
page after page.

So back to an autumn morning in the Isle of Wight. Past the
chalk scar on the hill which had the sun full in its face, along
the upland track which might have been an early road; to
watch the land give up all pretence at getting on with the season
and settle in favour of another motionless unalterable world
like the Golden Age. The faintest haze of mist, mistakeable for
heat, was making hay of distances and giving a new and awful
proportion to the cliffs below Tennyson Down. It seemed odd
to talk. Yes, there were worlds of higher being to which we
could aspire and which, sometimes without knowing it, we
reached; it was silly though comforting to give the name and
person of God to them. A disfigured rabbit with its heart
beating hopped away into a gorse bush, and there were carcases
torn by birds. Nothing could be explained in terms of logic,
and it was ridiculous to attempt it. It would be good to suppose
that one paid for the sin of a lifetime in a moment immeasurable
by our own standards of time, when the whole of the pain one
had caused was visited upon one after death. Down through the
golf course to Freshwater Bay, light glaring off the water; a
glass of beer. And as I sat there in the sun, at the end of a good
summer, I was already busy in my mind with certain final
sentences that would glow like autumn, glimmer like a calm
sea and eventually move away into silence on, if possible, a
dying fall.

A Select Bibliography

(Place of publication London, unless stated otherwise)

1918 THE CHAPMAN OF RHYMES. *Verse.*

1922 BRIEF DIVERSIONS, Cambridge. *Miscellany.*
PAPERS FROM LILLIPUT, Cambridge. *Sketches.*

1923 I FOR ONE. *Essays.*

1924 FIGURES IN MODERN LITERATURE. *Criticism.*

1925 THE ENGLISH COMIC CHARACTERS. *Criticism.*

1926 GEORGE MEREDITH. *Criticism.*
TALKING. *Essays.*

1927 ADAM IN MOONSHINE. *Novel.*
OPEN HOUSE. *Essays.*
THOMAS LOVE PEACOCK. *Criticism.*
BENIGHTED. *Novel.*
THE ENGLISH NOVEL. *Criticism.*

1928 APES AND ANGELS. *Essays.*

1929 FARTHING HALL. *Novel.* In collaboration with Hugh Walpole.
ENGLISH HUMOUR. *Criticism.*
THE GOOD COMPANIONS. *Novel.* Dramatised with Edward Knoblock, 1931.
THE BALCONINNY. *Essays.*

1930 THE TOWN MAJOR OF MIRAUCOURT. *Short Story.*
ANGEL PAVEMENT. *Novel.*

1932 DANGEROUS CORNER. *Drama.*
FARAWAY. *Novel.*

1933 WONDER HERO. *Novel.*
THE ROUNDABOUT. *Drama.*
ALBERT GOES THROUGH. *Story.*

1934 LABURNUM GROVE. *Drama.*
ENGLISH JOURNEY. *Commentary.*
EDEN END. *Drama.*

1935 DUET IN FLOODLIGHT. *Drama.*
CORNELIUS. *Drama.*

1936 SPRING TIDE. *Drama.*
The original edition was published as by George Billam and Peter Goldsmith, the latter being a pseudonym for J. B. Priestley.
BEES ON THE BOAT DECK. *Drama.*
THEY WALK IN THE CITY. *Novel.*

1937 MIDNIGHT ON THE DESERT. *Autobiography.*
TIME AND THE CONWAYS. *Drama.*
MYSTERY OF GREENFINGERS. *Drama.*
I HAVE BEEN HERE BEFORE. *Drama.*
PEOPLE AT SEA. *Drama.*

1938 THE DOOMSDAY MEN. *Novel.*
WHEN WE ARE MARRIED. *Drama.*

1939 JOHNSON OVER JORDAN. *Drama.*
RAIN UPON GODSHILL. *Autobiography.*
LET THE PEOPLE SING. *Novel.*

1940 THE LONG MIRROR. *Drama.*
POSTSCRIPTS. *Broadcast talks.*

1941 OUT OF THE PEOPLE. *Commentary.*

1942 GOODNIGHT, CHILDREN. *Drama.*
BLACK-OUT IN GRETLEY. *Story.*

1943 DAYLIGHT ON SATURDAY. *Novel.*
THE MAN-POWER STORY. *Commentary.*
BRITISH WOMEN GO TO WAR. *Sociology.*

1944 DESERT HIGHWAY. *Drama.*
HOW ARE THEY AT HOME? *Drama.*
THEY CAME TO A CITY. *Drama.*

1945 THREE MEN IN NEW SUITS. *Novel.*
LETTER TO A RETURNING SERVICEMAN. *Essay.*

1946 THE SECRET DREAM. *Essay.*
RUSSIAN JOURNEY. *Travel.*
BRIGHT DAY. *Novel.*

1947 THE ARTS UNDER SOCIALISM. *Lecture.*
MUSIC AT NIGHT. *Drama.*
THEATRE OUTLOOK. *Criticism.*

1947 AN INSPECTOR CALLS. *Drama.*
JENNY VILLIERS. *Short Story.*

1948 THE LINDEN TREE. *Drama.*
THE GOLDEN FLEECE. *Drama.*

1949 DELIGHT. *Essays.*

1949 THE OLYMPIANS. *Opera Libretto for music by Arthur Bliss.*
HOME IS TOMORROW. *Drama.*

1950 EVER SINCE PARADISE. *Drama.*
GOING UP. *Stories and Sketches.*
SUMMER DAY'S DREAM. *Drama.*

1951 FESTIVAL AT FARBRIDGE. *Novel.*

1952 DRAGON'S MOUTH. *Dramatic Quartet.* With Jacquetta Hawkes.

1953 TREASURE ON PELICAN. *Drama.*
MOTHER'S DAY. *Drama.*
THE OTHER PLACE. *Stories.*

1954 THE MAGICIANS. *Novel.*
LOW NOTES ON A HIGH LEVEL. *Novel.*

1955 MR. KETTLE AND MRS. MOON. *Drama.*
JOURNEY DOWN A RAINBOW. *Travel.* With Jacquetta Hawkes.

1957 THE ART OF THE DRAMATIST. *Criticism.*
THOUGHTS IN THE WILDERNESS. *Essays.*

Mr. Priestley's works, including *The Collected Edition, The Popular Edition,* and the Plays (except acting editions) are published by Messrs. Heinemann. Acting editions of various plays are published by Messrs. Samuel French.

Index